WEEKEND**escape**

BARCELONA

The spellbinding Catalan capital

Barcelona is a city of contrasts set between the mountains and the sea, a tireless reveler by night and hard-working by day, fervently European yet fiercely Catalan. *Seny* – common sense – and *rauxa* – a touch of madness – make it fluctuate between tradition and innovation. Loyal to its past, but ever reaching out toward the future, it combines imagination with a sharp nose for business.

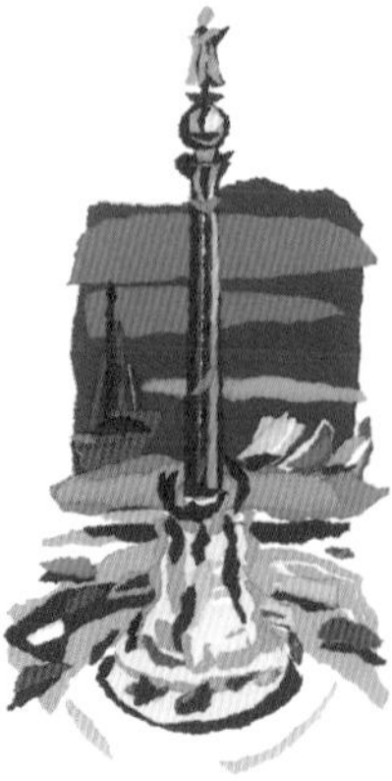

"It isn't possible to talk of one Barcelona, because Barcelona is made up of several distinct interwoven elements. Archeologists ought to know why eternal cities are made up of archeological layers, as if the place they chose for their existence was the result of a vague yet inevitable plan," observed Manuel Vázquez Montalbán in his work *Barcelonas.* Notable travelers of the 1930s, such as Joseph Kessel, and those associated with the Civil War, like George Orwell and Ernest Hemingway, wouldn't recognize the port areas of the city today. The slogan of the 1990s, "Make Barcelona Beautiful," inspired countless architectural projects, which have transformed this legendary former stronghold of resistance to Francoism. With the arrival of the Olympic Games in 1992, it was decided that Barcelona needed a face-lift, and with envigorating enthusiasm several of its old quarters were given a creative and well thought-out refurbishment.

The capital of Catalonia burst into frenzied action and museums, shops, restaurants, bars and galleries flourished. Modernity, creativity and the Catalan identity blended to produce a visual feast. From

old-fashioned town houses to the latest bars and from the traditional charm of a cabaret act in the Barrio Chino to the stunts of an acrobat on the Ramblas, you'll find yourself in the middle of a forward-looking city, full of life and color, but also proud of its past. Indeed, the people of Barcelona take their roots very seriously. Holidays and festivals follow on one from another in a whirlwind of tradition. Southern European in terms of their fierce pride and attachment to tradition, northern European in terms of their work ethic and business acumen, Catalans cultivate their identity as others cultivate their prize blooms – jealously and with great care.

As you wander through the labyrinth of narrow streets you may come across a delightful shaded patio concealing a collection of Picassos, or sit on the terrace of the Plaça del Pi and sip a *horchata* (barley drink) to the sound of an amateur saxophone player.

If you like to sample the food of a city as well as its atmosphere, try La Boqueria, the covered market located on the Ramblas, which is a riot of color and delicious smells, and everything a Mediterranean market should be. Try some dried fruit and nuts for a snack and then head for the port and the revitalized shoreline of Barceloneta. It is lined with trendy restaurants and designer bars where you can sample *copas* and *tapas* and watch families out for their Sunday afternoon consitutionals. Barcelona is a city that rarely sleeps. Catalans say with a superior air, that siestas are for Andalusians.

The nights are neon-lit, retro, rococo, sequined or high-tech. Adopt the Catalan mentality of work hard and play hard, and embark on a round of the bars. You'll need a lot of stamina and the ability to stay awake well into the small hours. The people of Barcelona certainly know how to enjoy life.

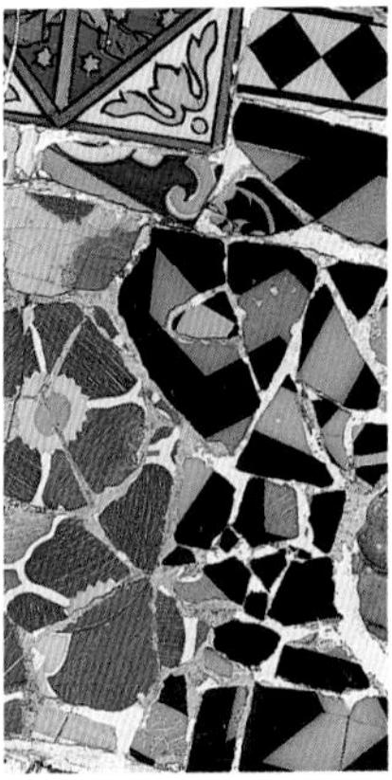

However, whether you're a party animal or prefer to stroll around admiring the architecture, you'll just love your weekend in Barcelona.

How to get there

The ideal seasons for visiting Barcelona are the spring and autumn. From March onward, you'll start to encounter the heat, but be on the lookout for frequent showers around Easter. Several big religious festivals light up the streets between March and June.

By plane

For a great weekend in Barcelona, the best way to get there is probably by plane. From the UK and Ireland, the flight takes approximately two-and-a-half hours. From the USA, Canada and Australasia, it is, of course, considerably longer and invariably requires a stopover, though there are some direct flights (see details opposite).

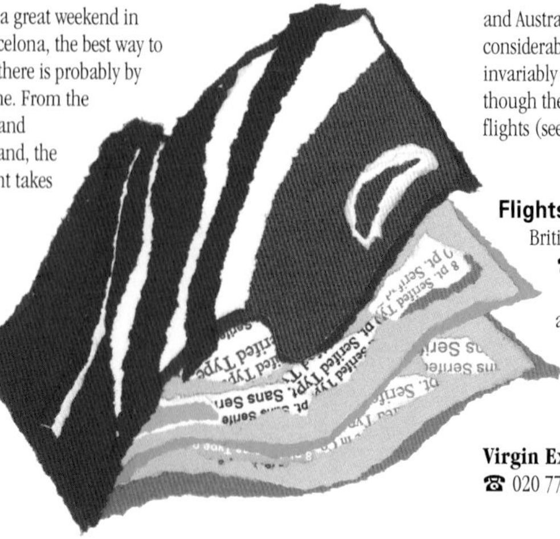

Flights from the UK

British Airways
☎ 0870 85 09 850
www.british-airways.com
Regular flights to Barcelona – call for schedules.

Virgin Express
☎ 020 77 44 00 04

WHEN TO GO?

Temperatures can soar to as high as 37°C/99°F in July and August, so avoid the summer months if you can't stand the heat and crowds of tourists. However, cultural activity is at its height in July, with the Greek theater staging musical entertainment and plays and bringing together foreign and Catalan companies. From August 15 for two weeks, Barcelona is the center for the traditional celebrations of Gràcia (see p. 16). September and October remain sunny and the Diada, the national holiday on September 11, is very enjoyable. If you do decide to go at the end of autumn or in winter, don't worry about the cold as the climate is still mild at that time of year, though temperatures can fall to below 7°C/45°F at night in February. You could also join in the celebrations at Christmas and New Year (see p. 14). On January 5/6 the Festa del Reis takes place – the Festival of the Three Kings, or the Three Wise Men, when children traditionally receive their presents.

www.virgin-express.com
Has flights from Heathrow, Stansted and Gatwick – all go via Brussels.

Iberia
☎ 0845 601 2854
www.iberiaairlines.co.uk
Has four flights a day from Heathrow to Barcelona and one from Manchester.

Easyjet
☎ 0870 6000 000
www.easyjet.com
Offer cheaper "no-frills" flights to Reserve in advance for the bargain fares.

Go
☎ 0870 607 6543
www.go-fly.com
Another low-cost airline which flies out of Stansted. Reserve well in advance for the best deals.

From Ireland

British Airways
☎ 1-890 62 67 47
www.british-airways.com
Offers flights from Shannon, Cork, and Dublin to Barcelona via London Gatwick.

Iberia
☎ 01-407-3017
www.iberia.com
Offers one direct flight per day from Dublin to Barcelona. Flights from other cities in Ireland go via Dublin.

From the USA and Canada

British Airways
☎ 7185 53 89 14
www.british-airways.com
Daily flights via London from all over the USA and Canada.

Delta
☎ 1-800-241-4141
www.delta.com
Has some direct flights to Barcelona via JFK. Call for more information.

Iberia
☎ 1-800-772-4642,
www.iberia.com
Offers direct flights – call for more information.

From Australia and New Zealand

There are no direct flights to Barcelona from Australia and New Zealand, but it's possible to stop over in other European cities, such as London, en route. Check with your travel agent for flight details or try looking on the web.

By train

From continental Europe, the train is also an option, though probably only if you're going for more than a couple of days, since it may require a night on board. The train journey from the UK can take up to 30 hours (see p. 6). Most international trains arrive in Barcelona at the Estació de França (metro Barceloneta). If you're arriving in Barcelona from within Spain, you'll arrive at Estació de Sants (metro Sants Estació). It's a long journey from the UK or Ireland and you'll need to allow between 20 and 30 hours. If you do decide to take the train, your trip will, of course, include crossing the English Channel, which you can do by ferry or by taking the Eurostar (☎ 08705 186 186 www.eurostar.com) to Paris. From there you could take the Trenhotel ("hotel train"), an overnight service offering sleeper accommodation. The journey takes just over 12 hours and you should ask at one of the rail companies listed about this service.

VOLTAGE

The electric current in Spain is 220 volts, as in most of the rest of Europe. Plugs have two round pins, so take an adaptor and a transformer if necessary.

European Rail
☎ 020 7387 0444 (UK)
www.europeanrail.co.uk

Rail Europe
Rail Europe Travel Center
178-179 Piccadilly, London W1
☎ 0870 584 88 48 (UK)
www.raileurope.co.uk
Or ask your travel agent for more information.

If you need information about rail services within Spain, call the national rail operator:

RENFE
☎ 90 224 02 02 (domestic)
☎ 93 224 34 02 (international)
www.renfe.com

By coach

The journey by coach can take up to a whole day, so it isn't really an option for just a weekend. However, you might consider taking a coach if you're going for a slightly longer break.

From the UK there are regular bus services to Spain. **Eurolines** (☎ 08705 143 219) has services to Barcel ona. Ask at major travel agencies, or visit their website at www.eurolines.co.uk for more information. Within Barcelona, buses usually arrive at Estació del Nord (metro Arc de Triomf), though some international buses arrive at Estació Sants.

Estació del Nord
☎ 90 226 06 06.

Estació Sants
☎ 93 490 40 00.

TAKING CARE OF YOUR BUDGET

Barcelona is no longer a particularly cheap destination. Spain, like Italy and Greece, is nowadays as expensive as any other European country. Hotel prices have also risen quite considerably in recent years and prices in the city inevitably tend to be higher than in the smaller towns. For two people, you should consider budgeting for around €150-200 a day for good accommodation, meals and outings.And if you really want the best deal available, make sure you ask for the "fin de semana" price (see p. 85), when you reserve your hotel room. You can expect to pay €18-36 for a meal, from €5-6 for a museum ticket, €0.85 for a bus ticket, €1.80-3.60 for a non-alcoholic drink, €6-12 for a disco, €15 for a concert seat, and up to €1.10 to send a postcard to Australia.

From the airport to the city center

The airport of Prat, 12km/7 miles south of Barcelona, is linked to the city by way of the Castelldefels motorway. There are various ways for you to get to the center.

By train

From 6am to 11.40pm, it takes 25 minutes to get to the Sants and Plaça de Catalunya station, with departures every half-hour. Tickets cost €2.16-2.50.

By airport bus

From 6am to midnight, a bus leaves every quarter of an hour for the Plaça de Catalunya, stopping at the Plaça d'Espanya and Plaça de la Universitat. Tickets cost €3.30 and the journey takes half an hour.

By taxi

For a cost of around €25, you can reach the city center in half an hour.

Airport information
☎ 93 298 38 38.

THE EURO

Since January 1 2002, the euro has replaced local currency in Spain and in many of the other EU countries. Before you leave, be sure to find out about the commissions charged on your credit card. Be aware that banks will also charge large commissions for using your check book.

SPANISH TOURIST OFFICES WORLDWIDE

UK & Ireland
22-23 Manchester Square
London W1M 5AP
☎ 020 7486 8077
Ⓕ 020 7486 8034
www.touristspain.co.uk.

USA
666, 5th Avenue, 35th floor
New York NY 10103
☎ 212 265 8822
www.okspain.org

8383 Wilshire Boulevard
Beverly Hills
Los Angeles CA 90211
☎ 323 658 71 88

845 North Michigan Avenue
Chicago IL 60611
☎ 312 642 1992

1221 Brickell Avenue
Suite 1850
Miami FL 33131
☎ 305 358 1992

Australia and New Zealand
c/o Spanish Tour Promotions Queen Street,
2-221 Melbourne
☎ 03 96 70 77 55
(For tourist offices in Barcelona, see p. 35).

WEBSITES

There are some good websites with plenty of tourist information. Try:
www.tourspain.co.uk
www.okspain.org
www.barcelona turisme.com
The first two websites offer detailed practical information on the whole of Spain and Tourspain, the website of the Spanish Tourist Board, also offers detailed information on Barcelona. Meanwhile the Barcelona Turisme site is ideal for checking out the latest news and events before you go.

Customs

In June 1999 duty-free allowances were abolished between EU countries, therefore EU citizens can take up to 800 cigarettes, 90 liters of wine and 10 liters of spirits when leaving Spain. If you enter Spain from a non-EU country, however, you can only take with you 200 cigarettes, 2 liters of wine, 1 liter of spirits and 60cl of perfume duty-free.

Formalities

EU citizens only require an identity card or passport. Citizens of the USA, Canada, Australia and New Zealand don't require a visa, just a passport.

Foreign embassies are all located in Madrid:

UK
☎ 91 700 82 00
Calle de Fernando el Santo

USA
☎ 91 587 22 00
Calle de Serrano, 75

Transport information
☎ 93 412 00 00.

LOCAL TIME

Spain is one hour ahead of GMT, except from the end of March to the end of September, when the difference is two hours. To sample the true Catalan lifestyle, you really need to adjust to the times of meals. Lunch is usually between 1.30 and 3pm, and dinner is eaten very late, at 10pm. Shops are generally shut between 2 and 4pm (see p. 96), and banks and museums are generally open all day (until 7 or 8pm) although some close between 2 and 4pm. The central post office is open from 8am to 10pm (see p. 34), and bars and clubs don't really begin to buzz until 1am in the morning (see p. 126).

Canada
☎ 91 423 32 50
Calle de Nuñde Balbao, 35

Australia
☎ 91 441 93 00
Plaza del Descubridor Diego de Ordás 3-2, Edificio Santa Engracia, 120

New Zealand
☎ 91 523 02 26
Plaza de la Lealtad, 2

Health and insurance

No vaccinations are needed for travel in Spain. EU citizens are entitled to basic health care in case of illness or accident. Make sure you obtain an EHIC form (available from UK post offices), which will enable you to recover any medical expenses you may incur while on your trip.
The *Barcelona Centro Medico* is responsible for helping foreign patients and will help with any medical problems and provide information on hospitals, doctors and dentists.

Barcelona Centro Medico
Avinguda Diagonal, 612, 2-14
☎ 93 414 06 43
Ⓕ 93 414 04 57
email: info@bcm.es
www.bcm.es (in English and Spanish versions).

It's important to take out comprehensive travel insurance to cover theft, as pickpockets are common in the city and thieves are amazingly efficient. Paying for your trip by credit card may cover you for some medical assistance and lost luggage, so check with your credit card company before you leave.

A taste of the sun
and the mountains

Like the country itself, Catalan cuisine has an authentic rustic flavor. The contrasting tastes of the Pyrenees and Mediterranean are combined in simple delicious dishes. Plain ingredients are simmered to conjure up substantial, nourishing fare, such as wild rabbit with prawns, beef stew with haricot beans, partridge with cabbage, cod with ratatouille, charcoal grilled snails with boletus mushrooms and many more dishes designed to tempt the appetite with all the mouthwatering aromas of Catalonia.

The basic ingredients: sauces and *pa amb tomàquet*

Catalan cuisine is generally prepared with olive oil or lard and uses a few basic sauces. *Picada* is made from almonds, garlic, pine nuts, walnuts, hazelnuts, oil, stale bread, warm water and chopped parsley ground in a mortar. *Sofregit* is made from finely chopped fried onions and tomato. *Samfain* is a ratatouille made from peppers, aubergines, tomatoes and sometimes onions. *Ailloli* contains just garlic, oil and salt. Simple but irresistible *pà amb tomàquet* (bread and tomatoes) accompanies meals It consists of a slice of toast rubbed with raw tomato and sprinkled with salt and a dash of olive oil (see **Casa Leopoldo**, p. 93).

A taste of the sun in winter

Escudella i carn d'olla is a tasty stew made from beef,

pig's ears and trotters, poultry, lamb, black and white *botifares* sausages, cabbage, celery, carrots, turnips, potatoes and haricot beans. To these are added *pilota*, a mixture of minced pork and veal combined with white breadcrumbs, eggs and spices. It's a typical regional dish that's prepared on cold days and always served in the Christmas season.

Mediterranean flavors

With one foot in the country and the other on the coast, Catalans appreciate the produce of both the mountains and the Mediterranean.

Aperitifs are served with shellfish *tapas* prepared with *tellines* and razor-shells (razor clams), fried red mullet and glass-eels, and grilled octopus and squid (see **Cal Pep**, p. 93). Or you can try *suquet de peix*, Costa Brava-style bouillabaisse, sea bream in a salt crust, *daurada a la sal*, and *arros negre*, black rice in cuttlefish ink, at **Set Portes** (see p. 57) or in the shade of a pine on the **Tibidabo hill** (see p. 65).

Throughout the year

Catalonia is generous with its produce in every season and the Catalans are especially fond of *cargolades*, traditional country dishes made from snails and meat grilled on vine branches and served with *ailloli*. In winter, the traditional *calçotada* unites family and friends with *calçots a la brasa*, leeks grilled over a wood fire, served with a sauce whose recipe is a closely guarded secret. *Butifarra negra*, or black pudding, is made from lean pork mixed with pig's blood. *Butifarra de l'Empordà* is sweetened and flavored with lemon peel and cinnamon using a recipe that dates back to the Middle Ages.

Tempting desserts

Of all the many mouth-watering desserts – crisp biscuits, spiced cakes and fromage blanc coated with honey and almonds – there's one, *crema catalana* or *cremada*, that's irresistibly smooth (see **Granja Viader**, p. 94). This delicious *crème brûlée* flavored with cinnamon is served with a misty glass of chilled *cava*. This local champagne is a specialty of the village of Sant Sadurni d'Anoia, where you can visit the Codorniù cellars in their magnificent *Modernista* setting.

CATALAN COOKING UTENSILS

If you long to emulate the locals in their cuisine, here are a few utensils you'll need to make tasty Catalan dishes successfully, together with the names of the shops where you can buy them. Paella dishes can be found at **Juan Soriano Raura** (see p. 111), while *olles*, the traditional olive and sand-colored terra-cotta cooking pots, salamander irons and ramekins for *crema catalana* (crème brûlée), and *porròs*, glass jugs with long spouts for drinking the local Pénédès white wine, can all be found at **Caixa de Fang** (see p. 112).

Copas, tapas and the rest

Barcelona is a city of cafés and bars. Some of them have already become the stuff of legend, while others are boldly avant-garde. In a city which boasts such a large variety of districts, each with its own distinctive character, you'll come across bars decorated with bric-a-brac, homemade distilleries with closely guarded secret recipes and *tapas* bars with ancient counters worn smooth by generations. There is something to suit everyone, from elderly domino players and veterans reliving past glories to the energetic and exuberant young.

Entertaining Catalan-style

Catalans don't readily invite people to their homes. As in many Mediterranean countries, people go out to socialize. An invitation *anar de tasca* or *ir de tapas* is seen as a mark of trust. You spend the evening going from bar to bar, never to get drunk but to meet friends informally over tempting snacks and a glass of the local wine.

Hot and spicy

The word *tapas* is said to come from the covers that used to be placed over glasses of wine to stop flies falling in (*tapar* means to close or stop). Once a piece of ham or cheese had been placed on the top it was only a short step towards creating the *tapas* we know today. The *tapas* menu is hugely varied, from *escalivada*, pickled aubergines and peppers in olive oil, to fried octopus, and from anchovies to the *embotits* (sausages and hams) of the Pyrenees. *Fuets*, dry sausages, sausage with black pepper and *pernil serrano*, a local ham, will all be on the menu.

Tapas etiquette

The *tapas* tradition is most firmly rooted in Andalusia and the Basque country and takes a slightly different form in Catalonia. You order *a la barra* (at the bar), *de raciòn* or *media raciòn* (a portion or half-portion) a little before dinner time (see p. 9), and avoid raising your voice to distinguish yourself from Andalusians, whom the Catalans consider far too noisy. People usually pay for their own drinks, although you can of course buy a round, if you're feeling generous.

Chiringuito and *bodega*

A *bodega* is a wine bar or inn, often decorated with casks and barrels to add a touch of local color. Drinks are served to order and it isn't uncommon for the wine list to also feature a selection of cold meats. The *can* or *casa* offers home cooking, with produce fresh from the market simmering on the stove. The waterfront *chiringuito* is a fishermen's restaurant, while the *fonda* is an inn where you eat whatever's in the pot. *Granjas* make delicious sweets from farm and dairy produce, while *horchaterias* specialize in barley water flavored with almonds or tiger nuts, *horchata de chufa*.

It could only happen here...

All sorts of activities are available in bars across Barcelona, especially games such as *Manilla*, Catalan tarot or the card game *subhastat*. Old men from the locality while the afternoon away using chickpeas or grains of corn as counters. Elsewhere there are book vending machines to salve your conscience.
At **La Bolsa** (see p. 128), drinks are quoted like on the stock exchange: their prices go up and down, depending on how successful they are.
The restaurant **El Japones** (see p. 129), with its smart, minimalist interior, attracts a young, trendy crowd.
At **El Salón** (see p. 129), in the evenings, pick the soup of the day or something from the regular menu.
One of the newer bars, **L'Arquer** (see p. 128), may have found the answer. It offers *copas y flechas*, which allows you to have a drink while brushing up on your archery skills.

LE MARSELLA AND FRANCO'S DICTATORSHIP

Le Marsella's (see p. 130) decor hasn't changed since it was founded in 1820 by a native of Marseilles as a place to drink absinthe. Since the turn of the 20th century the Lamiel family has presided here. During the fascist dictatorship, singing and meetings were strictly forbidden in the bar, and the writing on the tarnished mirrors still reads "*està prohibido cantar*" (singing prohibited). Here you can also have your cards read by a tarot expert.

Religious festivals and traditions

Throughout the year, religious festivals and traditions turn the city into an open-air theater. Popular culture is still very much alive, delighting crowds of onlookers with processions of papier-mâché giants. With Fellini-style cross-dressing at carnival time, interminable dancing of *sardanas* (see p. 17) and amazing balancing acts by *castellers* (see p. 16), these festivals are a very lively sight indeed. Each celebration is accompanied by special sweets and cakes and the shop windows are full of color. Barcelona is a festive city throughout the year.

December

From December 13 onwards, Santa Llucia's (St. Lucy's) Day, the cathedral square is covered with stalls on which tinsel, baubles, beads and ribbons evoke the atmosphere of Christmas. The crib figures are given a place of honor, displayed in a setting of bark and moss, but the presence of the *caganer* – a typical Catalan figure of a shepherd relieving himself – is a big surprise. He's supposed to be fertilizing the ground and is thus a fertility symbol. You can buy crib figures at **Rosès** (see p. 105).

January

To celebrate New Year' Eve, family and friends gather to eat the *postre del music* (musician's dessert) made of honey, dried fruit and *matò* (curdled milk). On the stroke of midnight, everyone eats 12 grapes for good luck in time with the chimes. During the night of January 5 to 6 small children leave pieces of *turróns* (nougat) and dried fruit for the Wise Men, along with bread and water for their camels. These same Wise Men

disembark at the port for the *Cabalgata de los Reyes Magos* (the Procession of the Three Wise Men). This is the most magical time of all for the children. They have already written out their lists of longed-for presents and treats, having handed them in to one of the pages who were in the city a few days earlier. The Wise Men now hand out the presents, but naughty children are only given a lump of coal.

February

From Shrove Tuesday to Ash Wednesday the *Carnestoltes*, carnival celebrations, which were banned for a long time under Franco, take place. On the last day they burn the effigy of a character embodying the carnival. There are masked balls and processions of floats in the streets of the city as well as in Sitges (see pp. 70-71). You can buy fancy dress at **Menkes** (see p. 105), an Aladdin's cave full of wonderful creations.

March

March 19 is San Josep's (St. Joseph's) Day, patron saint of fathers and carpenters, and a very popular Christian name throughout Catalonia. It's celebrated by eating *crema catalana* (see p. 11, buy the necessary cooking utensils at **Caixa de Fang** see p. 112). Palm Sunday opens Holy Week and on Rambla de Catalunya you can buy palm leaves woven into crosses, flowers, fantastic birds and so on. In the Mediterranean region, the palm tree is a symbol of regeneration and immortality On Easter Sunday godfathers give their godchildren a *mona*, a cake in the shape of a crown with several whole eggs set in it. The Easter egg represents life and perfection (buy them at **La Colmena** see p. 125).

April

Along with England, Catalonia celebrates Sant Jordi's (St. George's) Day on April 23. The patron saint had his hour of glory in the Middle Ages, when he slew a dragon. The Catalan

nobility adopted him as their emblem when they recaptured Catalonia from the Moors. On this day, a lover gives his sweetheart a rose and she in return gives him a book (**Sant Jordi** bookshop, see p. 123).

May

On May 11, the fair of Sant Ponç, patron saint of homeopaths, is a chance to buy medicinal and aromatic herbs. On Carrer de l'Hospital, stalls and stands are set up selling delicious syrups, candied fruit and honey to the delight of the sweet-toothed. Barcelona still has around 40 herbalist's shops with fragrant window displays dotted about the different areas of the city (see **Anormis** p. 41).

June

In June, *Corpus Christi* celebrates the Eucharist. Since 1264, Christianity has taken over ancient processions designed to ripen the corn, and *caps grossos* ("big heads" and giants) parade through the streets. In Barcelona, the tradition of the *ou com balla* (dancing egg) has taken place in the cathedral cloisters and patio of the Casa del Ardiaca since the 18th century. An empty egg is balanced on the jet of the fountain. For some people this symbolic association of water and birth has a profound religious significance. June 23 is St. John's Eve, when the summer solstice is celebrated with bonfires. In the past, people used to burn old objects and furniture at crossroads, as a sign of purification. Nowadays this is no longer allowed, except on Montjuïc Hill. Passing three times over the flames is said to protect you from evil and people share *coca*, pine-kernel cake sprinkled with *barreja*, a mixture of malmsey, muscatel and spirits.

July and August

During the summer months, the famous *castells* are erected, and every Catalan dreams of becoming a *casteller* of his town. The *castell* is the symbol of the community. For the townspeople, it means building a living castle by balancing one on top of another. Several volunteers form a muscular base onto which the rest climb. Groups compete to reach from five to nine levels. It's always a child, the *anxaneta*, who sets out to conquer the castle and waves to the crowd when he reaches the top. This Mediterranean tradition originated in ceremonies designed to celebrate the earth's fertility. On August 15, the festival of Gràcia starts and for around two weeks there's drinking and dancing in the streets of the former village, which is now part of Barcelona. The people of Barcelona are extremely proud of their local traditions.

September

Catalonia's National Day (*Diada*) falls on September 11 and commemorates the taking of Barcelona by Felipe V in 1714. Local institutions were then abolished and the day has become the symbol of nationalism. It's not the defeat of the city that's being celebrated, but the fight against the Bourbons. There's a good deal of Catalan flag waving on the *Diada*. On September 24, the *Festes de la Mercè* are dedicated to the Virgin Mary, who was made the patron saint of Barcelona in the 19th century. Since then, she's headed the bill at the *Festa Major*, when the city's inhabitants are in a kind of ferment, both secular and

religious. Delicious local produce is on offer on every street corner, while giants and dragons drive out evil spirits. During the week of September 24, people attend musical and theatrical performances in the Sant Jaume, Cathedral and del Rei squares, Plaça Reial and Escorxador Park.

November

All Saints' Day puts an end to the autumn festivities and celebration of abundance. Now it's time to remember the dead and turn fearsome beings into benevolent ancestors. In former times, on the eve of All Saints' Day, families would gather together to say rosaries for the dead while eating sweet chestnuts. The thick consistency of the chestnuts was supposed to block the way to roaming spirits, which people feared would try to take over the bodies of the living. Nowadays, you merely eat *panellets*, marzipan sweets covered in pine nuts in memory of the chestnuts, accompanied by a glass of sweet wine.

THE CATALONIAN LOCAL DANCE, THE *SARDANA*

The *sardana*, the quintessential Catalan dance, has very ancient, probably Cretan, origins. All generations take part in it and, after a brief introductory step, short eight-bar steps alternate with long 16-bar ones, repeated twice over. At the end, the dancers join hands in the center of the circle. The band, or *cobla*, consists of 11 musicians playing the *flabiol* (a recorder played with one hand), the tambourine, two cornets, a *fiscorn*, two *tibles* (wind instruments) and the *tenora* (oboe), the instrument that symbolizes the *sardana*. You can join in the dancing on Sundays at noon in the cathedral square and at 6.30pm in Sant Jaume Square (and you can buy your espadrilles for dancing at **Manual Alpargatera**, see p. 99).

A soccer crazy city

With the unifying slogan "More than a club," the legendary soccer team Barça has the loyalty of some 105,000 members, more than any other soccer club in the world. When Barça wins, flags fly, horns sound and there's singing in the streets. And if you casually mention the magic word Barça when talking to a Catalan, you'll score an immediate hit and any wariness will vanish in a flash.

The Barça soccer club

The club was founded in 1899, when Barcelona had aspirations of becoming an important capital. The Great Exhibition of 1888 had launched the city on its way and it was trying to become part of the European movement. Over a century has passed since the Swiss, Hans Gamper, founded this local institution. It's amusing to think that Barça, a symbol of the Catalan spirit, wears the red and blue of a Swiss province, and that the majority of the founder members were English or German.

A spirit of independence

Barça's matches against Real Madrid under General Franco were a focus for the hatred of centralism. Its financial strength – it's the richest club in Europe, with an annual budget of 31 million euros – and political attitude under the dictatorship constantly attracted enmity. Nowadays it remains the bastion of the Catalan spirit, combined with a desire to cross the Pyrenees in search of international recognition.

From north to south

As Gamper named the club after the city, the people of Barcelona feel a great affinity with their soccer team. The club has been instrumental in the integration of "immigrants" from other parts

of Spain. To be a *socio* (member) is in a way to become Catalan, by affiliation to a winning side. From the start, the founder members regarded the institution as a place of union and fraternity. It brings together people from every walk of life and membership cards are handed down from father to son.

Camp Nou

Inaugurated in September 1957, Camp Nou replaced the original and legendary Corts Stadium. A single stone from Corts Stadium became the foundation stone of the new stadium, thus ensuring continuity. Designed by three architects, Soteras, Mitjans and Barbòn, it can hold 120,000 spectators and is the second largest stadium in the world.

The Barça Club Song

A stadium filled with supporters is always an impressive sight and the Camp Nou echoing with the club song makes Barça a force to be reckoned with:

We are the reds and blues
(la gente blaugrana).
It doesn't matter where we come from,
North or south,
On this we all agree,
We're brothers under the flag,
Red and blue in the wind.
A cry of courage has made our name known throughout the world – Barça, Barça, Barça!'

The Fountain of Canaletes

There's a place in Barcelona at the top of the Ramblas where people gather to talk about sport. The Fountain of Canaletes, on the site of an ancient spring, was once the meeting-place of strangers passing through the city. Nowadays it's where the latest match against Real Madrid is discussed and soccer takes on

the air of a medieval joust. If you read a little Castilian Spanish buy a local daily, *la Vanguardia* or *el Periodico*, and, to complete the picture, dip into the famous novel by Manuel Vázquez Montalbán, *Offside* (published by Bourgois).

◂ AIR EUROPA DESPLAZA VUELOS A BARCELONA · PÁGINA 22 ▸

LA VANGUARDIA

Pujol fuerza a Aznar a tramitar como ley el decreto sobre TV

Tercer asesinato de ETA en menos de treinta horas

El Ajax ve a Van Gaal en el Barça

BARÇA MUSEUM

Avinguda Aristides Maillol, 7 ☎ 93 496 36 00
Open Mon.-Fri. 10am-6pm, Sat.-Sun. 10am-2pm
Entry charge.

The Barcelona Soccer Club Museum enjoys world fame for a museum of its kind and is the second most visited museum in the city. Photos, trophies, records and replays of match highlights portray the club's rich history. A biennial F.C. Barcelona art event brings together painters, sculptors and writers whose work is inspired by the sport. Thus artists such as Dalí, Clavé, Miró and Subirachs have added to the institution's prestige.

Antiques and old lace

Barcelona has a good choice of antiques shops and markets, so anyone who enjoys strolling around its narrow streets and ancient squares stands a chance of finding something interesting. A diligent search can uncover old *azulejos* (tiles), ceramics, cooking utensils, a betrothal chest (*caixa de nùvia*), or even an old edition of *Tintin* in Catalan. The flea market, Els Encants, is a good source for finds. It has a colorful sea of stalls with a mixture of old clothes and bric-a-brac.

Catalan furniture

From the Middle Ages onwards, Catalonia was linked to the rest of Europe by sea. Overland transport remained more difficult, and furniture from the rest of Spain seldom found its way into the region. It was as rare to own a Spanish leather cabinet, as it was a Chinese vase. Instead, furniture and other goods were imported from other countries such as England and France.

An air of provence

In times gone by, carpenters from Provence settled in Girona and passed on secrets of their trade. You'll come across a great deal of this *masia* (farmhouse) furniture made of walnut, sometimes inlaid with light boxwood. Often, for reasons of economy, the front of the furniture was elaborately worked, while the back was left rough. Over the centuries carpenters worked in oak, walnut, silver birch, poplar and even mahogany imported from overseas.

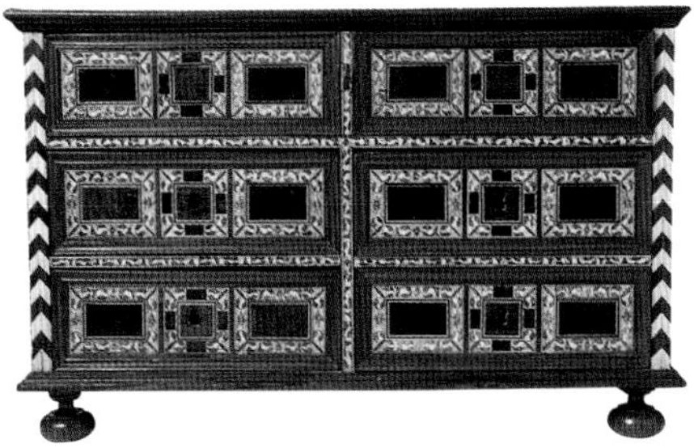

The *caixa de nuvia*

The betrothal chest was an institution in Catalan families from the 16th to the 18th century. Generally made of walnut, it was around 140cm/55in long and 60cm/24in high and was used for storage. It spread from the plains to the mountains and became common in both

farmhouses and palaces. On their wedding day, the betrothed couple were each given a chest containing their dowry. The woman's had a small door, which opened to reveal a jewel compartment. In the 18th century, this traditional chest gave way to a chest of drawers, then a mirrored wardrobe, less mobile, but more practical for storing belongings.

From antiques to *azulejos*

Antiques lovers should make their way to the Call, the old ghetto of medieval Barcelona (see p. 41). The streets of Banys Nous and Paja are lined with antiques shops. At 8 Paja, they sell a fine selection of walking sticks with ivory, mother-of-pearl and silver knobs, as well as sumptuous ostrich-feather fans and vases made of glass similar in style to that of Gallé. At 11 Paja, Erika Niedermaier sells delicate 17th-century ceramics with metallic detail, apothecaries' ointment pots and a wide variety of wrought-iron objects, whose history this devoted collector will be only too pleased to tell you. At 22 Banys Nous, Maria José Royo specializes in sacred art, gilded wood, popular sculpture, and interesting and unusual Baroque liturgical objects. At 14 Banys Nous, there are items of early Catalan furniture, betrothal chests and lovely old *azulejos* (a word derived from the Persian *'al zuleich'*, meaning a smooth flat stone), colorful enamelled tiles typical of the Iberian Peninsula (see p. 115).

L'ARCA DE L'AVIA, THE STUFF OF DREAMS

Carrer dels Banys Nous, 20 ☎ 93 302 15 98
Open Mon.-Fri.
10am-2pm, 5-8pm,
Sat. 10am-2pm.

Founded in 1840, these famous suppliers to the Spanish royal family made bobbin lace and Spanish *mantillas*. At that time, such delicate accessories were highly prized and, as with jewelry, the amount a woman wore was a sign of her wealth. This shop is a treasure chest *(arca)* of everything that once made up a bride's trousseau – embroidered linen tablecloths and sheets, damask bath towels and even the ceremonial cloth in which the dowry was sometimes placed.

Modernisme – exuberance and extravagance above all

Barcelona is renowned for its superb Modernista architecture. From the Palau de la Música and hospital of San Pau to the Quatre Gats bar and Bolòs pharmacy, this artistic movement shaped houses like sculptures, covered façades with azure and gold, and added floral designs to chimneys. Everything defies logic and order, and imagination rules supreme. On every street corner, you come face to face with the spirit of inventiveness and unusual detail that makes this city so fascinating.

A family likeness

Modernisme refers to a cultural movement that emerged at the end of the 19th century. It had similarities with the British Modern Style, Belgian 1900 Style, German Jugendstil, Viennese and Prague Sezessionstil, Italian Liberty and French Art Nouveau. It became famous because of its appropriation of the powerful *Renaixença* (1878), or the movement for a return to the Catalan identity. Writers, musicians and poets added their efforts to those of painters and architects to turn Modernisme into a lifestyle.

At the turn of the 20th century

In the 19th century, people believed that progress and science would be the saviors of humanity. However, at the turn of the 20th century, this thinking underwent a serious crisis, triggering anarchy and assassination attempts, and Barcelona was nicknamed "The Rose of Fire." Subjectivity, irrationality, a return to nature and oriental doctrines overtook order and reason. Modernisme was a reaction to academicism and provincial bad taste. Sustained by the profits of industrialization and commerce, Modernisme found patrons in the wealthy inhabitants of Barcelona.

The roots of Catalan art

The desire to return to its origins was rooted in the desire to review the glories of the Catalonia's past and her achievements. In England, at the same time as this, the Pre-Raphelite Brotherhood (1848), the Arts and Crafts Movement (1888) and Symbolism were promoting

spiritual art with a social purpose. The designer William Morris (1834-1896) relaunched the craft industry taking inspiration from nature, while in France Viollet-le-Duc (1814-1879) became fascinated by medieval bulidings.

How to recognize the *Modernista* style

In the 19th century, eclectic architecture dominated the scene and buildings were a mixture of styles. They could display Egyptian, Roman, Moorish and Greco-Roman influences, as the university, (see p. 54), while the neo-Gothic style was also an unqualified success. *Modernista* architects distinguished themselves by the use they made of these sources of inspiration. Sinuous lines, asymmetry, dynamism, richness of detail and refinement were all of great importance.

From street lights to shop signs

Modernisme regarded a design as a "total work" integrating all the arts. It could be the result of collaboration between cabinetmakers, craftsmen in mosaics, ceramicists, jewelers, craftsmen in wrought iron, sculptors and master glass-makers, all driven by attention to detail. From door handles to mosaic cladding, everything was carefully designed. Take a look at the hallways of *Modernista* buildings and appreciate the wealth of decorative detail used.

Keeping the ladies happy

Barcelona still has some 200 shops and clothing stores dating from this era, which were designed with women very much in mind. You can picture elegant ladies, dressed in velvet or damask choosing fabric for a new outfit, or selecting from the very latest, fashionable accessories. Some

women would tie their ankles together in order not to tear the delicate fabric of their tight skirts, so it would appear that being a fashion victim is by no means a new thing...

IN PURSUIT OF MODERNISME

Wake up and have breakfast at the **Hotel España** (see p. 89). Go for a walk and shop for delicious chocolates at **Antiga Casa Figueras** (see p. 51), rare stamps from **Monge** (see p. 116), and made-to-measure shirts at **Xancò** (see p. 50). Take a leisurely lunch on the terrace of **El Asador de Aranda** (see p. 92) or a coffee at **Quatre Cats** (see p. 29). In the afternoon, visit the **Museu d'Art Modern** (see p. 57) and stop for a drink at **Hivernacle** (see p. 57), pop into the **Palau Macaya** (see p. 119) for a temporary exhibition, and in the evening go to a concert at the **Palau de la Música** (see pp. 42-43 and 134). Also very interesting is the **"modernist circuit"** (information at the tourist offices, see p. 35).

Total design

"Make Barcelona beautiful," the slogan of the 1990s triggered an avalanche of innovative projects. Barcelona wanted to improve its appearance, and exploring it on foot you'll discover open-air sculptures, smart traffic signs and state-of-the-art phone booths that amount to a kind of street art. From comic strips to coat hangers, nothing escapes this creative fever, and modern designs and the traditional Catalan identity combine to stunning effect.

An ancestral tradition

Catalonia is at the cutting edge of Spanish design, but why here more than elsewhere? When the New World was discovered, the Catalan people were harassed out of any form of trade with the Americas whatsoever. They never profited from the crock of gold that the Americas became and so devoted all their efforts to developing their own strengths and resources. The result of this inward concentration of effort was a strong tradition of family cottage industries that has lasted throughout the centuries.

Ideas, but no raw materials

Like all countries lacking in raw materials (Japan, Sweden and Switzerland, for example) Catalonia specialized in light manufacturing – textiles, glass, ceramics, leather, metallurgy, wood, paper and the graphic arts.

Modernisme (see p. 22) advocated the idea of the "total work," arguing that an architect ought to be able to produce the whole design, both outside and inside.
This concept of symbiosis between raw materials and interior design was revived in the 1950s by the generation of architects that included Oriol Bohigas, Josep Antoni Coderch and designers such as André Ricard and Oscar Tusquets.

The designers – Jacks-of-all-trades

It isn't easy to classify the artists who move from one discipline to another – from architecture to interior design, by way of fashion, ceramics and even graphics.
Most representative of them all is perhaps Xavier Mariscal, the prodigious young designer of ceramics, posters, comic strips, wardrobes, shoes and carpets. His mascot for the Olympic Games, "Cobi," has become an international star, just as its creator.

Design organizations

After 40 years of Francoism the city has once more taken up its creative vocation. Today there are seven schools of design, and many design bodies. The oldest and most prestigious organization is the FAD (Foundation of the Decorative Arts), which awards an annual prize to the best designer.
Caixa, one of the biggest Spanish banks, is an outstanding contributor, providing ever-present support for science and the arts, continuing a very Catalan turn-of-the-20th-century tradition of patronage (see the Güells, pp. 30-31).
In addition to this, every two years in April, the city organizes a "Design Spring," a tour of galleries, shops and bars to make sure its inhabitants are ready for all the latest trends when the good weather starts.
For more information, call ☎ 93 218 28 22.

Catalan specialties

If you want to get into Catalan design, there's plenty of choice – formal furniture by Mariscal and Cortès, an armchair with a "Mantis" wooden shell by Pep Bonnet, Mariscal furnishing fabric by Marietta or his "duplex" stool with colorful wavy feet.
More sober and timeless is the TMC lamp (1961) by Milà exhibited at the MoMA, or the Lluscà pressure cooker.
All these designs have the distinctive feature of playing with different styles and influences (Italian in particular) to invent a brand new style of their own, involving a concern for detail, materials and humor, and producing enormously creative designs that have stood the test of time.

TOTAL DESIGN

The shop **BD** (Carrer de Mallorca, 291, metro Verdaguer) is a happy blend of varying design styles all under one roof. It's located in **Casa Thomas,** a Modernista building designed by by Domènech i Montaner (1895), its purpose being to show an outstanding selection of the century's designs – furniture designed by Gaudí, Le Corbusier and Frank Lloyd Wright, together with contemporary pieces by André Ricard, Ricardo Bofill and Philippe Starck. Don't miss it.

Fashionable designers

Barcelona has always had a reputation as being a haven for artists, and this is still as true as ever. Gaudí and Mariscal are well-known names, but few people have heard of the city's new young designers. It's as if those outside Barcelona still think design here is frozen in the 1980s. Nothing could be further from the truth – the city is buzzing with innovative and often surprising examples of creativity.

Searching for authenticity

The 1980s saw a real creative boom in Barcelona. Design was the new watchword of the city, and conversations invariably began with the question: "Are you a designer or do you have a real job?" The 1990s saw a marked move toward a more honest interpretation of design, which gradually became authentic rather than trendy, minimal rather than complicated and far more accessible to the general public. The use of natural materials and simple lines and forms became the order of the day.

Special jewelry creations

If you are tired of the usual gold bangles, pearl necklaces and paste earrings that you find in most jewelers, then you may find the creations of the new Barcelona designers more interesting. **Karin Wagner** creates unusual pieces in lightweight felt. Her earrings and rings, produced in a range of subtle colors, are quite stunning. **Ana Hagopian** is yet another champion of unusual materials. Her pieces are real works of art, made from folded recycled paper, glued, cut and painted by hand. **Chelo Sastre**'s jewelry is made using rather more classic materials, but still based on recycled products. She has spent many years refining her designs, which are soft and sensuous. **Clara Uslé** also deserves a mention after the successful launch of her first collection in 1999. She has become a master at applying color and motifs onto silver and gold.

Cozy interiors

Lovers of interior design will be seduced by the creations of various newcomers on the Barcelona scene. Simplicity is the key once more, in a range of items such as cutlery, crockery and home furnishings. **Nani Marquina**'s rugs combine form, texture and color and are both elegant and contemporary in design. **Estudi Eulalia Coma** produces wonderful crockery, particularly the Blau Pics range with the patterns concentrated around the edge. Today's young artists have also not forgotten the children. **Virginia Pulm**'s pieces are decorated with patterns that look as if they have been designed not only with children in mind but by the children themselves.

Stylish and elegant clothes

Fashion designers don't just clothe women, they pay homage to them with creations in silk, velvet, linen and pure cotton. **Lydia Delgado**, a former classical ballet dancer from Liceu, is now one of the top designers in Barcelona. **Ruth**, on the other hand, is focusing her talents (for the moment, anyway) on children's clothing. Her simple embroidered motifs are based on the natural world – insects, animals and plants – and are quite unique.

Antonio Miró

Antonio Miró has been designing clothes for both men and women for 25 years, so why place him in this category of young designers? Every season Antonio reinvents himself, constantly reinterpreting classic fashion designs. His clothes are well cut, impeccably finished, simple but stylish and produced in natural fabrics. As much as anything, it is his attention to detail that distinguishes him from the rest of the crowd.

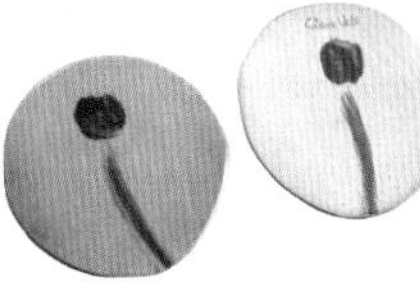

WHERE TO FIND TODAY'S DESIGNERS

Karin Wagner
Forum (see p. 98).
Lydia Delgado
See p. 100.
Antonio Miró
See p. 55.
Chelo Sastre
At Hipòtesi (see p. 101) and Moska (see p. 45).
Nani Marquina
Carrer Església, 4-6
☎ 93 237 64 65.
Clara Uslé
At MNAC (see p. 68) and the Fondació Joan Miró (see p. 68).
Ana Hagopian
At Forum (see p. 98), Hipòtesi (see p. 101) and Moska (see p. 45).
Virginia Pulm
At Vinçon (see p. 54).
Estudi Eulalia Coma
At Vinçon (see p. 54).
Ruth
Biscuit
Boulevard Rosa (Paseo de Gràcia Rambla Cataluña, 66
☎ 93 215 81 70.

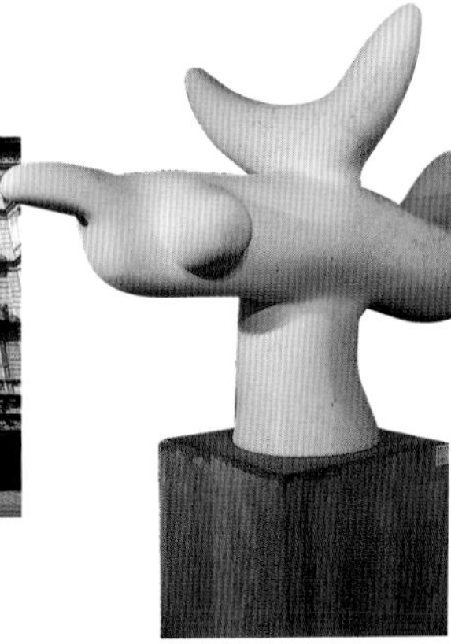

Miró, Picasso and Tàpies

Barcelona is synonymous with the genius of three great artists, Miró, Picasso and Tàpies. Each in turn was inspired to produce images of the city in keeping with his own particular vision. Miró transformed the world into a riot of colors and shapes, Picasso sketched locals and peasants with just a few strokes, while Tàpies experimented with collage and engraving techniques.

Joan Miró

Born in 1893 in a small street in the heart of the Ciutat Vella (Old Town), Miró always remained very attached to Catalonia. He became an artist of international renown, but never forgot his homeland. His first exhibition was held in 1918, after which he divided his time between Spain and France. The **Fundació Joan Miró** (p. 68) is a good way to see his work. Look for sculptures, lithographs, etchings, tapestries, ceramics, theater sets and masks. The city is littered with monuments bearing his signature.
To complete your whirlwind study you can also see exhibits of his work at the **Museu de Ceràmica** and then try a cocktail at **Boadas** (see p. 50), a bar which he regularly frequented.

Pablo Picasso

Born in Malaga, Picasso was barely 14 years old when he arrived in Barcelona in 1895. He lived here for seven years before settling in Paris in 1904. His formative years were spent in a turn-of-the-20th-century climate much influenced by Modernisme (see p. 22). His studies of the

Les Demoiselles d'Avignon

Barceloneta, the dissident fringes of the Barrio Chino and his first Blue Period works (**Museu Picasso**, see p. 43), reflect the misery pervading the Barcelona of 1900.
He lived with his parents in the Plaça de la Mercè and studied at the **Llotja** Art School (see p. 44). Later he took a flat at 36 Nou de la Rambla and frequented the variety cafés of the Barrio Chino or El Raval, the city's red-light district.
The title of his famous painting *Les Demoiselles d'Avignon* (1906) was inspired by a brothel in the Carrer d'Avinyó frequented by sailors from the neighboring port.

Antoni Tàpies

It's difficult to separate the life and work of this artist born in 1923. All his creativity was channeled toward the service of the political. He was influenced by the Dadaist and Surrealist movements and turned his art into a free-thinking, provocative game. He developed an abstract style which looked deceptively simple, including the use of symbols as a kind of sign language, and incorporating everyday objects in his work. Tàpies produced his first major pieces in 1945. For a thorough appreciation of this artist visit the **Fundació Antoni Tàpies** (see pp. 53-54). Then visit **Ediciones T** (see p. 119), the art gallery founded in 1994 by his son, which specializes in graphic works and books. It also makes a point of exhibiting young Catalan and foreign talent.

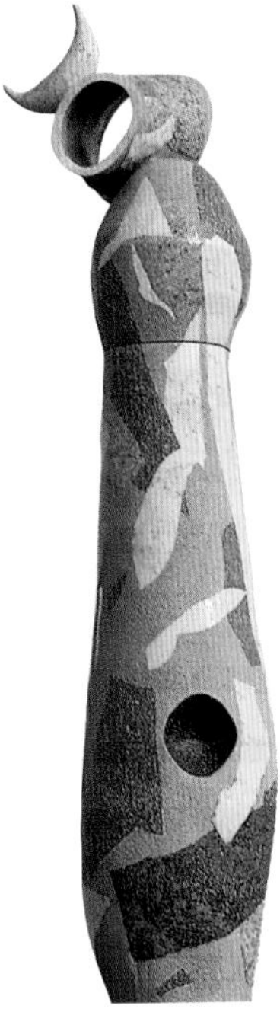

QUATRE GATS CAFÉ

C. Montsiò, 3 ☎ 93 302 41 40. Closed Sun. lunchtime.
This café opened in 1897 on the ground floor of a neo-Gothic building designed by the *Modernista* architect Puig i Cadafalch. The name Quatre Gats is probably a tribute to the Chat Noir (Black Cat), a Parisian cabaret that Pere Romeu, one of the founders of the Quatre Gats, knew from having worked there.
From 1897 to 1903, the Quatre Gats saw gatherings of the artists and writers of the day. Picasso designed the menu and held his first exhibition here in 1900.

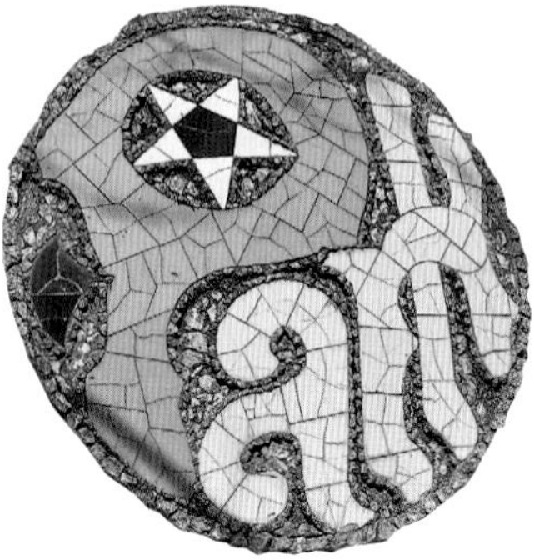

Gaudí:
Utopia with a heart

Antoni Gaudí is an architect inseparable from our image of Barcelona. Both visionary and iconoclast, he is the embodiment of this surprising and intoxicating city. Born in 1852, he was a fervent nationalist and misanthropist, and very devout. Towards the end of the century, with the cultural and political rebirth and a new economic prosperity, the enlightened middle classes were eager to adopt the new European trends and Gaudí profited particularly from the patronage of wealthy industrialist Eusebi Güell.

Parc Güell

Between 1900 and 1914, Gaudí wanted to create a garden along the lines of an English park, as a contrast to the growing industrialization of the city. His sponsor, Eusebi Güell (see box opposite) was preoccupied with utopian social reforms. The area was originally barren and Gaudí refused to have the ground leveled and subjected his designs to the demands of the landscape. Slanting supporting columns make the paths look more like tunnels. (To reach Parc Güell, take the metro to Vallcara, walk to the open-air escalator and ride to the top.)

Chameleon-like architecture

At times, confusion sets in and it's hard to tell where Gaudí's designs begin and where nature ends. His work merges, chameleon-like, with the very ground on which it is built. Gaudí drew inspiration from many sources, but beneath an apparently haphazard exterior, his work is very well planned, and the fantastic shapes were designed with the help of detailed models. The area was supposed to have been divided up into 60 parcels of land for housing, but only two were ever built, one of which is now the Gaudí museum. The project was never completed as Güell was afraid it would eat up his entire fortune. Today, the two houses at the entrance to the park look like gingerbread houses, strange palaces built from odds and ends – hallucinogenic mushrooms with Moorish outlines and bold mosaics.

Successful integration

Further into the park a multicolored salamander stands guard, while at the top a square edged by a long winding bench, with backrests in the shape of the human form, overlooks the city. Josep Maria Jujol, Gaudí's assistant, collaborated with him on the project. They used broken ceramics as decoration reviving the Arab tradition of *azulejos* and thus preceding the Dadaist and Cubist collages.
Whatever your artistic preferences, a walk through this amazing park is a must. There is nothing like it anywhere else in the world (Carretera Carmel ☎ 93 284 64 46. Open every day 10am-6pm in winter, 9am-8pm in summer).

La Sagrada Família

The first stone of this church dedicated to the Holy Family was laid in 1883. Like the Sacré-Coeur in Paris, it was built with the help of donations from the public. Its design and building occupied Gaudí for 40 years. Sadly only the east façade depicting the life of Christ was finished before Gaudí's untimely death in 1926, when he was killed by a tram. Unfortunately in 1936 all Gaudí's plans were destroyed by the Anarchists and so his designs could never be carried through to completion.
However, work began once more toward the end of the 1950s, causing great contoversy, and still continues to this day under the watchful eye of Jordi Bonet.
This building is an exuberant flight of fantasy. Eight towers twist upwards into the sky, an extravaganza in stone that everyone can appreciate for its boldness, no matter what their individual tastes and preferences may be.
Another "must" on your visit to the city. (Carrer Mallorca, 401 ☎ 93 207 30 31, F 93 476 10 10. Open every day 9am-6pm in winter, 9am-8pm in summer. Entry charge.)

THE GÜELL FAMILY

Juan Antonio Güell used to boast that all the "good families" of turn-of-20th-century Barcelona came to his house in Pedralbes – aristocrats, the wealthy upper middle-classes, the "nouveaux riches" and *indianos* with legendary fortunes. The latter group, to which the Güell family belonged, symbolized success, social climbing and prestige in the Spanish colonies. On their return to the city, they started a textile business and built palaces and parks. Eusebi Güell, the son of the founder of the line, became Antoni Gaudí's patron and commissioned many projects from him.

Practicalities

On one side you have the Sierra de Colserola and, on the other, the blue Mediterranean – two unmistakable landmarks that make it easy to find your way in Barcelona. When Catalans give an address, they always also say whether the street number faces the mountains or the sea. Traffic flows freely in the Eixample, where the avenues are dead straight. Only the old quarters are narrower, but the steeples of the cathedral, Santa Maria del Mar, and of the del Pi church will help you get your bearings. Don't be afraid to explore the labyrinth of medieval alleyways in the old town – you won't get lost for long and it's the best way to really get to know the place. So go ahead – a fascinating city lies waiting for you!

Getting around Barcelona

Visit the old quarters (Raval, Ribera and Gótico) on foot and stroll around them at your leisure. The Eixample, criss-crossed by a network of wide avenues, is served by a number of bus routes and metro stations. The numerous taxis are among the cheapest in the European Union. You'll need them for going to the Güell Park and the Sagrada Fam lia, which are not in the city center.

Public transport information
☎ 010 or 93 318 70 74

BY BICYCLE OR ROLLER BLADES

At weekends, Barcelona residents frequently rent bicycles or roller blades to ride or skate along the waterfront or Diagonal. It's the ideal place for cycling enthusiasts and those who enjoy unusual walks. At Coche Meny, Carrer Esparteria 3, open every day ☎ 93 268 21 05, you can rent a bicycle for €5 an hour. Bicycle tours are organized on Saturdays, Sundays and holidays. Bicycle rental is also available on the Diagonal near the Corte Inglès, and at the Vila Olimpica.

Lost property
Calle Ciudad, 9 (Metro Jaume I) ☎ 010 or 93 402 70 00
Guardia Urbana
This is a service reserved for tourists in the event of theft, accident or loss of documents:
La Rambla, 43
☎ 93 344 13 00
Open 24 hours a day.

The metro

Air-conditioned and clean, it runs from 5.30am to 12pm on Monday to Thursday, Sunday and holidays, and until 2am on Friday and Saturday. This is the fastest form of transport in Barcelona. In addition there are a few FGC (Ferrocarrils de la Generalitat de Catalunya) suburban city rail lines which link up with the metro, the most useful of which goes to the Tibidabo. Signs with the letter 'M' in a red diamond indicate the entrance to the metro stations. Signs for RENFE or FGC indicate a link with the national railway system or the Catalonian system. Tickets cost €1.10, but for the duration of your stay it's worth buying a T1 ticket (€5.80), which entitles you to 10 journeys by bus and metro. You're restricted to traveling on the metro with the T2 ticket. In addition, there are one-day (€4.40), three-day (€11.30) and five-day (€17.30) travel passes for bus and metro. You can buy a pass (also available for two or four days) from the ticket office of the Universitat and Sagrada Família stations, or from the tourist offices of the placa. de Catalunya and of the Sants train station. Important intersections on these lines are Passeig de Gràcia, Catalunya and Diagonal.

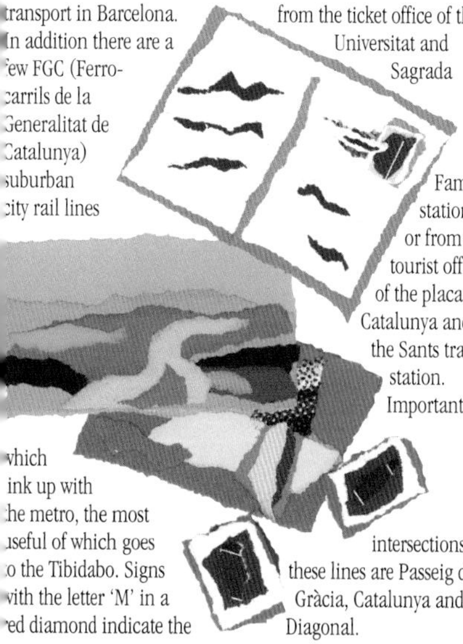

Buses

Numerous bus lines cover the whole city. Buses operate from 6am to 11pm, and some continue right through to 4am (Nitbus). You can tell which are which by their numbers and can consult the maps on bus shelters that give details of their routes. The Tomb bus is the most useful;
it goes from Catalunya square to Pius XII square. Although more expensive, it runs every 5 to 10 minutes. There also exists a Tibibus running at half-hour intervals between the plaça de Catalunya and the pl. de Tibidado, starting from 11am on weekdays and 10.30am on weekends. Two Bus Turístic buses (one red, one blue) offer a 3.5-hour tour of the city (two itineraries: north and south). They leave from the plaça de Catalunya, every 20 minutes, between 9am and 8pm. Adult fare: €14.

By car

If you rent a car for the weekend, be very careful about where you park it. It will cost you €90 to free it from the city car pound. When you do find a space, which is not easy, don't leave any valuables in sight as thefts are commonplace. Daytime parking lots are reasonably safe (around €1.50 per hour, €20 a day).
Avis
Carrer de Còrsega, 293-295
☎ 93 237 56 80
☎ 93 298 36 00 (at airport)
www.avis.com

Europcar
Gran Via de les Corts Catalanes, 680
☎ 93 302 05 43
🅕 93 317 35 59
www.europcar.com

Hertz
Calle Tuset, 10
☎ 93 217 80 76
Ⓕ 93 237 29 20
www.hertz.com

Taxis

The city is swarming with 11,000 yellow and black taxis. The green light shows they're available. They are still very reasonably priced and rarely refuse to take you, even for very short distances. Over 1,000 taxis accept credit cards. Allow €1.50 for the pick-up charge (€2.90 if you phoned for a cab). A supplement is charged for luggage, airport transfers and animals.

Barnataxi
☎ 93 357 77 55
Radio Taxi
☎ 93 225 00 00

By train

To get to Sitges (see pp. 70-71), take a train from Passeig de Gràcia station (RENFE station) or Sants station. Air-conditioned trains operate every 15 minutes from 5.30am to midnight and the journey to this charming seaside resort takes 35 minutes. Don't forget to date stamp your ticket, otherwise you risk getting fined. For all information, visit www.renfe.es.

Making a phone call

The international country code for Spain is 34. The code for Barcelona is 93. When dialing a local number from within Barcelona you must also ensure that you dial 93 at the beginning – the codes were changed in 1998, making the old seven-digit numbers nine digits. All the numbers in Spain now have nine digits and you must dial all nine from wherever you are calling. Public telephone booths have a distinctive modern design and are blue and green in color. Calls are very expensive, and you'll never have enough coins to make an international call. It's much better to buy a *tarjeta telefónica* (phone card) for €6-12, at an *estanque* (tobacconist's). Failing this, try the **locutorios telefonicos**, pay phones installed at Sants station, open Mon.-Sat. 8am-10.30pm, Sun. 9am-10.30pm.

Writing home

Oficina Central
Plaça Antoni Lopez
☎ 90 219 71 97
Metro Barceloneta or Jaume I
Open Mon.-Fri. 8am-8.30pm, Sat. 9.30am-2pm.

The impressive main post office is located at the lower end of the Via Laietana. To send a postcard within Europe costs €0.50, and a postcard or letter weighing up to 20gm costs €0.72 to USA or Canada and €1.10 to Australasia. You can buy stamps from a tobacconist's. *Bústies/buzones* (mailboxes) are easy to spot – they're large with yellow lettering and are found at crossroads.

MUSEUM OPENING TIMES

Museums are generally open from 10am until 8pm, except on Sundays, when they close at 2pm, and on Mondays, when they're closed all day. One exception: the Tàpies Foundation (which closes at 8pm on Sundays) and the Pedralbes monastery, which closes every day at 2pm. Opening hours remain the same throughout the year, except at the Olympic Gallery. Entrance costs between €3 and €6 per person. Certain tickets will give you access to several museums. Find out before buying your ticket, or use the Barcelona Card (see below). *La Guía del ocio* can be purchased from kiosks, a useful guide to current exhibitions, concerts and shows. It also contains precise and valuable information about the visiting hours and temporary closures of the town's monuments.

Tourist information offices

Turisme de Barcelona
Rambla de Catalunya, 123
☎ 93 368 97 00,
93 368 97 30
or 906 30 12 82 (if you're calling from Spain)
Ⓕ 93 368 97 35
www.barcelonaturisme.com
Open Mon.-Fri. 9am-8pm.

This is the address of the administrative office, which is closed to the public. It can be useful, however, if you want to get hold of a Buyer's Card (see p. 97) or to order documentation in advance of your stay in Barcelona. Otherwise, for maps and information, it's better to visit one of the following tourist offices (ask for the special brochures on Miró, Modernisme, Gaudí, new urbanism, the Golden Quadrat…). You can also buy a highly convenient Barcelona Card: free public transportation, discounts (up to 50 percent) on selected museums, restaurants and shows. The staff speak several languages and are very helpful. For an adult, the card costs €16.25 per day, €19.25 for two days, €22.25 for three days, etc.

At the airport:
Aeropuerto del Prat
08820 Barcelona
☎ 93 478 05 65
(Terminals A and B)
Open every day 9am-9pm.

At Sants station:
Plaça de Països Catalans
08014 Barcelona
☎ 93 368 97 30
In winter open Mon.-Fri. 8am-8pm, Sat., Sun. and public holidays 8am-2pm. In summer open every day 8am-8pm.

On the Ramblas:
Palau de la Virreina
La Rambla, 99
☎ 93 301 77 75
Open Mon.-Sat. 10am-8pm, Sun. 11am-3pm.

On Plaça Sant Jaume:
(Ground floor of City Hall in the Gothic Quarter)
Open Mon.-Fri. 9am-8pm (from 10am Sat.), Sun. and holidays 10am-2pm.

On Plaça de Catalunya:
Open every day 9am-9pm
www.bcn.es
From June to September, hostesses wearing red and white uniforms and "i" badges are assigned to strategic points to provide useful information for tourists.

What to see in Barcelona
and sights not to miss

The following is a selection of the 12 most beautiful sites in Barcelona, including museums, churches and parks.

The Town's History Museum

Take a journey into the everyday life of ancient Barcelona. Relive 2,000 years of the city's history by walking through one of Europe's largest underground archeological museums.
See Walk 1, pp. 40-41, and Don't Miss, p. 72.

The Picasso Museum

To discover or rediscover the work of this extraordinary painter, nothing can compete with a visit to the magnificent palaces which house the Picasso Museum.
See Walk 2, p. 43, and Don't Miss, p. 73.

The Museum of Contemporary Art

From its architecture to its temporary exhibitions, this museum is a tribute to Barcelona's thriving art scene.
See Walk 3, p. 47 and Don't Miss p. 74.

The Catalan National Museum of Art

The MNAC is a treasure-trove of medieval art, particularly recommended to amateurs of Gothic and Romanesque art.
See Walk 10, p. 68, and Don't Miss p. 75.

The Tàpies Foundation

The foundation's primary focus is the work of the Catalan artist Antoni Tàpies; its research center also gives a fascinating insight into 20th-century art.
See Walk 5, pp. 53-54, and Don't Miss, p. 76.

The Thyssen-Bornemisza Collection

The Pedralbes monastery exhibits an important part of the fabulous Thyssen-Bornemisza collection, bringing together mostly religious works of the greatest artists from the 13th to the 20th century (Fra Angelico, Velásquez and Rubens, among many others).
See Walk 9, p. 65, and Don't Miss, p. 77.

The Joan Miró Foundation

The foundation's collection of works by Joan Miró is simply extraordinary. Don't miss the gardens and the terrace, where the artist's sculptures and a stupendous view of Barcelona await you.
See Walk 10, p. 68, and Don't Miss, p. 78.

The Sagrada Família

Love it or hate it, you cannot avoid a visit to this symbol of Barcelona, Antoni Gaudí's most famous and extraordinary achievement. Prepare yourself for a surprise!
See p. 31, and Don't Miss p. 79.

The Cathedral

Dedicated to St. Eulàlia, one of the town's two patron saints, the cathedral is the city's center of religious feasts and traditions.
See Walk 1, pp. 38-39, and Don't Miss, p. 80.

Santa Maria del Mar

Sober and elegant, this Catalan Gothic sanctuary is one of Barcelona's finest churches. The Ribera district in which it was built also has considerable charm.
See Walk 2, p. 43, and Don't Miss, p. 81.

The Palace of Music

Part of the UNESCO's Heritage of Humanity since 1997, this edifice was built on the ruins of an ancient monastery in the Sant Pere district. Its concert hall is bathed in light that pours through its magnificent stained-glass windows.
See Walk 2, pp. 42-43, and Don't Miss, p. 82.

The Güell Park

A haven of peace and greenery, the fairy-tale Güell Park reveals the multiple facets of Gaudí's talent. In the heart of this fantasy world stands the Casa Museu Gaudí, where the artist lived 20 years.
See pp. 30-31 and Don't Miss, p. 83.

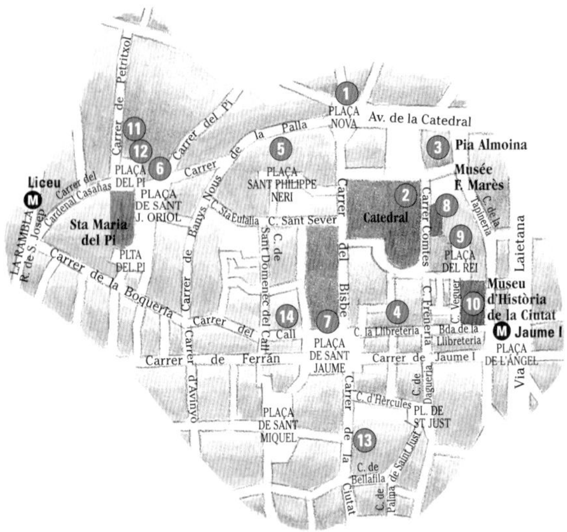

The Barrio Gótico:
in the shadow of history

The Barrio Gótico lies at the heart of the old town. It's a maze of narrow 14th- and 15th-century alleyways into which the sun does not always manage to penetrate. Full of little shops, cafés and bars, it's a "must" on your visit to the city. After wandering around its elegant squares and museums enjoy some refreshment in the plaça del Pi and try a *tortilla* washed down with *horchata* (barley drink).

❶ Plaça Nova★★

The ancient city of *Barcino,* whose name is carved in the square, was founded here. The remains of the 4th-century city walls contain two Roman towers flanking the del Bisbal Gate. One of them has a hollowed-out niche dedicated to St. Roch, the patron saint, whose feast day is celebrated in summer on August 16. There is also an antiques market on Thursdays, Advent celebrations, and *sardana* dancing on Sundays. The 18th-century Baroque façade of the bishop's palace adds cachet to the setting. The same can't be said of the College of Architects built in 1961, though it does have a frieze by Picasso.

❷ Catedral★★★

**☎ 93 310 25 80
Open every day 8am-1.15pm, 4.30-7pm.
Free entrance for the catedral.
Entrance charge for the terrace, the museum and the choir. (visits: 1.30-4.30pm)** **See p. 80**

The magnificent Gothic façade actually dates from the 19th century. The cathedral is dedicated to St. Eulàlia and was founded in the 13th century and completed in the 15th. It contains precious liturgical objects, such as the famous 16th-century *Christ of Lepanto* crucifix, said to have been on board the Spanish flagship of Don Juan of Austria at the time of the decisive victory against the Turks in

1571. The baptismal fonts are believed to have been used to christen the first six Indians brought back by Christopher Columbus in 1493. The delightful cloister is planted with orange trees, magnolias, medlars and palm trees. It's a cool oasis and a haven of peace that is sometimes broken by the cries of 13 geese, their number symbolizing Eulàlia's age at the time of her martyrdom.

❸ Pia Almoina and Diocesan Museum★★

Avinguda de la catedral, 4
☎ 93 315 22 13
Open Tue.-Sat. 10am-2pm, 5-8pm, Sun. 11am-2pm.
Entry charge.

This medieval institution next to the cathedral was once an almshouse providing a hundred poor people a day with a meal. Its subtle conversion to a Diocesan Museum is very successful, and is well worth climbing the few steps for.

❹ Catalonia Excursion Center★★

Carrer del Paradis, 10
Open Tue.-Sat. 10am-2pm, 4-8pm, Sun. 10am-2pm.
Entry free.

You're treading on the remains of the Roman city here. A mill wheel embedded in the ground marks the entrance to the site. At the summit of *Mons Taber*, a temple dedicated to Augustus, built in the 1st century, was visible from far away. The columns you see today were found at the start of the 20th century, while the bells of the nearby cathedral are a reminder that gods have been worshipped on this mound for thousands of years.

❺ Plaça de Sant Felip Neri and Shoe Museum★★

☎ 93 301 45 33
Open Tue.-Sun. 11am-2pm, closed Mon.
Entry charge.

This shady little square, often bypassed by visitors short of time, occupies the site of a former cemetery. The Baroque façade of the church and two 16th-century houses form a harmonious group. The emblems of the Guilds of Shoemakers and Coppersmiths – the lion of St. Mark and two spoons – are clearly visible. In the Shoe Museum, you can't miss the foot measuring 1.22m/4ft that was used as a model for the Christopher Columbus monument.

6 Plaça del Pi and church★★★

Open every day 9am-1pm, 5-8.30pm.
Entry free.

The del Pi church is a perfect example of 14th-century Catalan Gothic. The square with its single pine tree (*pi*) is delightful. In summer, sit on the terrace, sipping iced coffee to the sound of a saxophone.

In winter, during Advent, the façades sparkle with a thousand lights. A slightly Bohemian air gives the place its charm.

7 Plaça de Sant Jaume★★

The institutional center of the city that was once the site of the forum, the public square in Roman times. The name *Jaume* (James) comes from the church that stood here until 1824. Today the Town Hall (*Ajuntament)* and Province of Catalonia (*Generalitat)* are in political opposition here. On feast days (Sant Jordi's and Sant Mercé's, see pp.14-17), the *castells* – pyramids of acrobats – defy the laws of gravity, while the flags of Spain, Barcelona and Catalonia flutter in the breeze.

8 Museu Frederic Marès★★★

Plaça St. Iu, 5
☎ 93 310 58 00
Open Tue.-Sat. 10am-7pm, Sun. 10am-3pm.
Entry charge except on Wed. from 3pm and the 1st Sun. of the month.

In fine weather, pause on the patio, where tables and refreshments await you. The museum houses Spanish sculpture from the Middle Ages to the 19th century. If there are

too many versions of *Virgin and Child* and *Descent from the Cross*, for your liking, go upstairs and see the fascinating collection of briar pipes, fob watches, pince-nez, parasols and fans.

9 Plaça del Rei, Saló del Tinell and Chapel of St. Agatha★★★

☎ 93 315 11 11
Open Jul. to Sep., Tue.-Sat. 10am-2pm, 4-8pm, Sun. 10am-2pm.
Entry charge.

This is the most remarkable group of buildings in the city. Climb the palace steps to reach the Saló del Tinell, the magnificent hall and throne room, built in the 14th century. It is here in this very room that the Catholic King

Ferdinand and Queen Isabella, on a visit to Barcelona, received Columbus on his return from the New World in 1493. On the walls, 13th-century frescoes illustrate this period of Catalan grandeur. The 14th-century palace chapel of St. Agatha is adorned with a renowned 15th-century painting, the *Constable's Altar-piece*, by Huguet. From the top of King Marti's turret you can see a maze of alleyways overlooked by a cluster of steeples.

⑩ Museu d'Història de la Ciutat★★

Plaça del Rei
Combined entry ticket includes the Saló del Tinell.

This museum, dedicated to the history of the city, is housed in the beautiful 15th-century mansion, Casa Clariana-Padellas. You can see extensive Roman ruins discovered during work carried out in the 1930s and the remains of a Christian basilica.

⑪ La Granja Dulcinea★

Carrer Petritxol, 2
☎ 93 302 68 24
Open daily 9am-1pm, 4.30-9pm.

A *granja* is a bit like a tea room, where fresh farm produce takes pride of place. Highly recommended is the *suisso con ensaimada*, thick hot chocolate topped with whipped cream and accompanied by tempting Mallorcan cakes and pastries, all beneath the understanding eye of the old man in the photo pinned to the wall. Don't worry, everyone in Barcelona, young and old alike, indulges themselves here.

⑫ La Gavineteria Roca★★

Plaça del Pi, 3
☎ 93 302 12 41
Open Mon.-Fri. 8.45am-1.30pm, 4.15-8pm, Sat. 10am-2pm, 5-8pm.

La Gavineteria Roca sells bladed instruments of all kinds. There's been a knife grinder here since 1911,

specializing in cut-throat razors, manicure sets, scissors, knives and penknives. The folding *navaja de Albacete* with a curved handle will cost you around €12. Note the extraordinary stainless-steel *Modernista* shopfront.

⑬ Anormi★★

Carrer de la Ciutat, 3
☎ 93 302 30 04
Open Mon.-Fri. 9.30am-1pm, 4-8pm.

Entering this, one of the oldest shops in the old town, you may well come across the very cure you've been seeking for ages. Señor Anormis acts as herbalist, doctor, confidant and adviser to his customers, and his formulae are only revealed in the strictest confidence.

⑭ THE CALL

The Call (alley) or ghetto conjures up one of the most flourishing facets of medieval Barcelona, the *aljama*, or Jewish community. Nowadays finding any trace of it requires a vivid imagination. The bloody pogrom of 1391 ended in fire and bloodshed. Now nothing remains but memories of the ambassadors, interpreters, financiers, astronomers, alchemists and eminent doctors who lived and worked here. Only carreres del Call, Sant Ramon del Call and Sant Domènec del Call still bear witness to the past.

2

The Ribera: past meets present

Living in the Ribera is like living in a village. Old crafts rub shoulders with fashionable institutions. The shop window of a humble upholsterer vies with the fashionable Galeria Maeght. Trendy designers work alongside glass-blowers, while the city's pensioners play cards. The streets are steeped in history, and are not only home to the church of Santa Maria del Mar, but also to the tea rooms and bookshops. One of the last fashionable quarters of the city, it's not to be missed.

P. Picasso: Las Meninas

❶ Palau de la Música★★★

C. de Sant Francesc de Paula, 2
☎ 93 295 72 00
Open daily, 10am-3.30pm
Guided tour (charge) every 30 minutes (phone in advance). **See p. 82.**

Built in 1908 in the pure *Modernista* style by Domenech i Montaner, this concert hall has superb stained-glass windows, mosaics and

;culpture, with an elaborate açade supported on three large :olumns. The accoustics are xcellent, and it's worth asking ιt the box office to see if any 'educed tickets are available ɔn the night of a concert.

2 Museu Picasso★★★

Carrer Montcada, 15-23
☎ 93 319 63 10
Open Tue.-Sat. 10am-8pm, Sun. 10am-3pm.
Bookshop and restaurant.
Entry charge. **See p. 73.**

Since 1963 the Palau Berenguer d'Aguilar has ιoused the works of Pablo Picasso. It opens onto one of ıe most aristocratic streets in he city. The Palau is a fine xample of the patrician tructures of the late Middle ιges, inspired by northern taly. The terra-cotta jars on

ıe ground floor, used for :oring oil, wine and water, how that the original ıhabitants were involved in :rade. On the first floor, some f Picasso's youthful works voke his brief, but intense ncounter with Barcelona's ohemian set. The room evoted to his interpretation of elásquez's famous painting *as Meninas* is the highlight f a visit to the museum.

3 Museu du Tèxtili i d'indumentària★★

Carrer Montcada, 12
☎ 93 310 45 16
Open Tue.-Sat. 10am-6pm, Sun. 10am-3pm.
Entry charge.

This museum, housed in the Palau de Los Marqueses De Llió, is a Gothic masterpiece whose original structure has been preserved. You can sample some homemade pastries on the patio before seeing the collections. Spread over two floors, the Textile and Costume Museum traces the development of textiles over a period of 1,500 years, with precious Coptic cloth, Chantilly lace, embroidered damask, beautiful *mantialls* (scarves), Indian calico, and creations by Worth and Balenciaga. Also on display are Catalan textile industry tools. Before leaving the palace, buy a few meters of fabric designed by Mariscal (€21.05 a meter/yard), the king of Barcelona design.

4 Santa Maria del Mar★★★

Plaça Santa Maria
Open every day 9am-1.30pm, 4.30-8pm.

Located on the waterfront, the church was originally called Santa Maria de las Arenas (of the sands). This early 14th-century Gothic building symbolizes the prosperity of the merchants of the period. Many sail-makers, stevedores and porters are buried in its walls. Built over half a century with remarkable unity of style, it has a wide nave and narrow aisles. In the Middle Ages Catalan sailors set sail for distant conquests to the cry of *Santa Maria*, their patron saint.

5 Passeig del Born★★

The Born, location for a market in medieval times, which sold goods from overseas including spices and

medicines, has a grisly past. Heretics condemned to death by the Spanish Inquisition were burned at the stake here. The Born was later turned into an open-air theater and jousts (*bournar*), tournaments and other knightly celebrations took place. In 1874, the Mercat del Born was erected, a metal-structured market hall, nowadays used for temporary exhibitions.

❻ La Lotja★

Plaça del Palau, 22
Open Mon.-Fri. 10.30am-1pm.

La Llotja market was a typically Mediterranean institution, and very powerful. Originally, this market hall was open to the elements, but in 1380, as business prospered and trade increased, a permanent building was erected. The *Consulat del Mar*, linked to the community of Catalan merchants overseas, was established here. Rebuilt in the 18th century, the low Gothic hall now houses the Stock Exchange and Academy of Fine Arts.

❼ Pla de la Garsa★

Carrer Assaonadors, 13
☎ 93 315 24 13
Open Mon.-Sat. 1.15-5pm, 9pm-1am, Sun. 9pm-1am.

A short distance from the Picasso Museum, this wine bar has the charm of an old-fashioned *bistrot*. A broken tiled floor surrounds the bar made of *rajoles* (terra-cotta tiles) from Valencia. The wrought-iron spiral staircase is the pride of the owner, who'll recommend the *embotits i formatjes*, an excellent selection of cold ham and

ewe's cheese washed down with a Rioja or Penedès wine (around €15).

❽ Galeria Maeght★

Carrer Montcada, 25
☎ 93 310 42 45
Open Tue.-Sat. 10am-2pm, 4-8pm.

Aimé Maeght (1906-1981) opened this Barcelona temple to contemporary art in 1974. Housed in the 15th-century Cervellò palace, it exhibits works by Kandinsky, Braque, Miró and Tàpies, as well as less well-known artists such as Bennassar, Grau and Solano. You can purchase art books, graphic works by talented young artists and even special collector's editions here.

❾ La Casa Gispert★★★

Carrer Sombrerers, 23
(☎ 93 319 75 35
Open Mon.-Fri. 9am-1.30pm, 4-7.30pm, Sat. 10am-2pm, 5-8pm.

Since 1851 the Gispert family have been *Mestres Torradors*, past masters in the art of coffee-roasting. From the gleaming black-and-gold shop front wafts the sweetish aroma

Wassily Kandinsky at the Galeria Maeght

of saffron, cinnamon and Ethiopian coffee. Sacks and ars overflow with dried fruits and spices as in an Oriental narket. In the back shop, the old almond-grilling oven s still going strong. A delightful way to ndulge the senses.

⑩ L'Euskal Etxea★

'laceta de Montcada, 1-3
☎ 93 310 21 85
Open Tue.-Sun. 12.30-3.30pm, -11.30pm.

'or *tapas* fans this restaurant offers a typical Basque election, including *txakas* (crab mayonnaise), *pimientos del piquillo* (green peppers) and mussel kebabs, accompanied by a local white *xacoli*, which are all the rage. This is a charming, typically *Euskera* (Basque) restaurant, which also houses a cultural enter.

⑪ Ici et Là★★

'laça Santa Maria el Mar, 2
☎ 93 268 11 67
Open Mon. 4-8.30pm, Tue.-Sat. 10.30am-8.30pm.

his is a simple yet ophisticated shop opening nto a square cooled by the spray from a Gothic fountain. Small pieces of iron furniture, multicolored mosaic tables and ethnic objects mingle with the creations of young designers, which include brightly colored tablecloths with contrasting traditional Catalan designs (a pair of tea towels costs €9.30).

⑫ Moska★★

Carrer dels Flassaders, 42A
☎ 93 310 17 01
Open Tue.-Sat. 10am-5pm. Closed Mon. & Sun.

The name of this small boutique pays tribute to Calle Mosca, which meets at an angle with Calle Flassaders, famous for being the city's narrowest street. The owner of the shop sees her jewelry as a collection of small sculptures, and exhibits them as if they are on display in a museum. The beautiful pieces are arranged in meticulously planned window displays designed by her architect husband. Here you'll find ancient pieces from Asia and Africa on sale alongside more contemporary works in such diverse materials as gold, silver, paper, resin, plastic and wood.

⑬ REC CONTAL

The tanning and dyeing industries were set up on the banks of the stream that gave this street its name. The street names of the Ribera evoke the ancient crafts which were practised in them: *Assaonadors, Blanqueria, Corretger, Vidrieria, Corders, Carders, Argenteria, Flassaders* and *Esparteria* (tanning, tawing, welding, stained-glass window making, rope-making, carding, silversmithing, blanket-making and working with rushes). The shopkeeping mentality was born here and the Catalans have a nose for business.

3

The Raval:
venture outside the old city walls

Better known as the Barrio Chino, the Raval has fascinated artists for a long time, with its pimps and prostitutes, transvestites, shady deals and more than a whiff of sleaze from the nearby port. For some years now though cultural institutions have been moving in, adding a touch of respectability to the area. It's a cosmopolitan mix of locals and immigrants from Africa and Asia.

❶ Centre de Cultura Contemporánia de Barcelona (CCCB)★★

Carrer de Montalegre, 5-7
☎ 93 306 41 00
Open Tue., Thu., Fri. 11am-2pm, 4-8pm, Wed. and Sat. 11am-8pm, Sun. 11am-7pm. Entry charge.

A perfect example of the new living alongside the old. Built in 1714 on the site of a 14th-century convent, this former asylum and workhouse is now home to the CCCB and is used for exhibitions of town planning. The superb patio (1714) and the façade (1993) harmonize well. At the back there is a lovely little café with a terrace.

2 Museu d'Art ;ontemporani★★★

ʾlaça dels Angels, 1
Vletro Catalunya
☎ 93 412 08 10
)pen Mon., Wed.-Fri.
1am-8pm (7.30pm in
vinter), Sat. 11am-8pm,
;un. 10am-1pm
:ntry charge. **(See p. 74).**

:he museum, known as
ΛACBA for short, was designed
y the architect Richard Meier,
ery much a fan of whiteness
ınd purity. This striking
uilding is an absolute
ontrast to the nearby façades
f the old buildings. Opened
n 1995, it displays a good
election of work by mainly
;atalan and Spanish artists
ince 1945, though there is
ome foreign work too.

3 Hospital de a Santa Creu★★

;arrer del Carme, 47-49/
;arrer de l'Hospital, 56
atio open every day
0am-6pm.

'ake a walk in the shade of
1e former 15th-century
ıospital garden, once a refuge
or pilgrims in Catalonia.
'he vestibule of the Casa de
;onvalescencia is sumptuously
ecorated with ceramic scenes
n green and yellow of the life
f St. Paul. Gaudí died here
n 1926.

4 Monasteriò Sant ʾau del Camp★★

;arrer de Sant Pau, 101
☎ 93 441 00 01
)pen Tue.-Sat. 7.30-
.45pm, Sun. 9.30am-
.30pm.

o escape the hustle and bustle
f the street, step inside Sant
au, the 12th-century
omanesque Benedictine
ıonastery where you'll be
ruck by the tranquility of the cloister. The parish priest will gladly give you an account of its history, if asked.

Inside the Palau Güell

5 Palau Güell★

Carrer Nou de la Rambla, 3-5
☎ 93 317 39 74
Open Mon.-Sat. 10am-2pm, 4-8pm. Entry charge.

This enigmatic palace was built in 1888 by Gaudí for his patrons, the Güell family. A tour of the building takes you through a turn-of-the-20th-century interior with Gaudí's curved and twisting shapes, while the façade displays his supreme artistry in wrought-iron work. The architect's fervent nationalism is apparent in the form of an eagle holding the coat of arms of Catalonia.

6 El Indio★

Carrer Carme, 24
☎ 93 317 54 42
Open Mon.-Sat. 10am-2pm, 4.30-8pm.

This is certainly one of the most attractive *Modernista* shopfronts in the city. The decor hasn't changed much for years, with colorful remnants of cloth displayed on wooden racks.

7 Pla dels Angels★★

Carrer de Ferlandina, 23
☎ 93 443 31 03
Open every day 9am-midnight (closed Sun. pm and Tue. lunchtime).

During the summer months, this restaurant stretches as far as the museum square. It's popular with a young crowd and you can enjoy a pleasant meal at reasonable prices in a relaxed atmosphere.

BARRIO CHINO

The Barrio Chino, or Chinese quarter, owes its name to a report by the writer Francis Carcoi entitled 'China Town', yet you won't find a trace of Chinese immigration here. The district has been inhabited by Andalusians since the beginning of the 19th century. Immigrants from Pakistan and Africa arrived recently to join them, making the Barrio Chino a kind of Catalan melting-pot.

4

The Ramblas: to see and be seen

Las Ramblas lies at the heart of the city and cuts through the old town. The most famous street in Barcelona is lined with cafés, bars, shops, hotels and newspaper kiosks. It's always busy, no matter what hour of day, though evening is undoubtedly the liveliest time. In the morning little old ladies clutching string bags trot from the market to the Betlem church. In the evening three-card tricks, artists selling paintings and improvised acrobatics extract money from passersby.

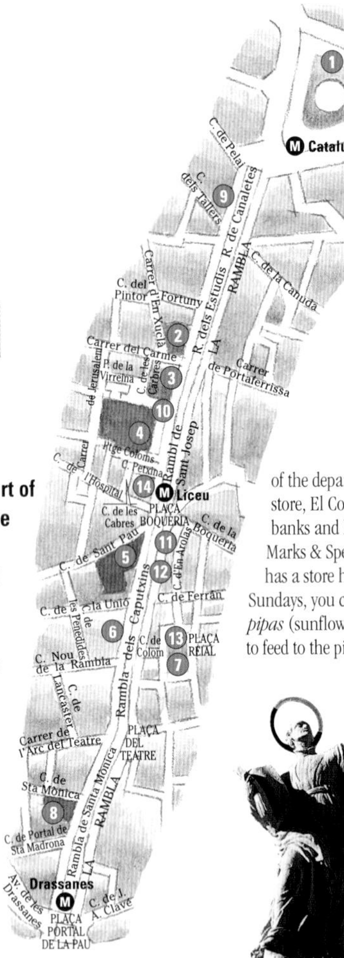

❶ Plaça de Catalunya★

This large and irregularly shaped square is the link between the old town and 19th-century Eixample, and was first landscaped in 1854. It became the nerve center of the city in 1925 with the building of the department store, El Corte Inglès, banks and hotels. Marks & Spencer now has a store here. On Sundays, you can buy *pipas* (sunflower seeds) to feed to the pigeons.

❷ Església de Betlem★★★

La Rambla, 107
Open every day 7.45am-9pm.

The façade of this church is a Baroque flight of fancy, with tatues of St. Ignacio de Loyola nd St. Francisco de Borja leep in conversation. Begun in 681, it formed the nucleus of complex of buildings ccupied by the Jesuits until heir expulsion in 1767. Sadly, he interior was gutted by fire luring the Civil War in 1936. n the morning the low angle f the sun casts a theatrical ight on one of the city's finest aroque monuments.

3 Palau de la Virreina★★★

as Ramblas, 99
☎ 93 301 77 75
pen Tue.-Sat. 2-8pm, un. 11am-3pm.
ntry charge.

Named after the Vicereine of eru, who lived here after the leath of her husband, this is a raceful 18th-century addition o the district. It later became he site for exhibitions of the lecorative arts. Take the main taircase to see the superb rench-style decor.

4 Mercat de la oqueria★★★

as Ramblas, 85-89
pen Mon.-Sat. 6am-.30pm.

troll round this covered narket which dates from 1860 nd and enjoy the wonderful Mediterranean feel. The locals hatter as they go round

selecting the day's best buys and

the stallholders call out to customers. The displays of fresh produce are really quite something to behold. If you wish to blend in with the locals, stand at the *barra*, the bar, of the *Pinocho* kiosk and sample the Catalan-style tripe.

5 Gran Teatre del Liceu★

Las Ramblas, 51-59
☎ 93 485 99 14
www.liceubarcelona.com
Tours: 11.30am, noon, 1pm
Guided tour: 10am.

The opera house, a symbol of 19th-century middle-class and industrial Barcelona,was built in 1844 and burned down for the first time in 1861. It was rebuilt before suffering a bomb attack. It went up in flames again in 1994, but has again been restored.

6 Hotel Oriente★

Las Ramblas, 45
☎ 93 302 25 58
Metro Drassanes

This hotel was built on the site of the Franciscan College of St. Bonaventura, of which only the old cloister was preserved. In its heyday notable people such as Ernest Hemingway stayed here, as well as various Hollywood stars and toreadors. In the 19th century it was still one of the biggest hotels in Europe and in 1975 Antonioni filmed *The Passenger* here with Jack Nicholson.

7 Plaça Reial★★

Under the 19th-century arcades is a fascinating mix of cafés selling *calamares a la romana* (squid), dealers selling "*chocolate*" or hashish, stamp dealers at the Sunday morning market, palmists, artists and tramps, with the odd policeman keeping a watchful eye. The terrace of the **Quinze Nits** (see p. 93) is a good place from which to

view the proceedings. Watch out for the street lights which are the work of a youthful Gaudí.

❽ Santa Monica Art Center★

Las Ramblas, 7
☎ 93 412 22 79
Open Mon.-Sat. 11am-2pm, 5-8pm, Sun. 11am-3pm.
Entry charge.

In 1988 Pinon and Viaplana converted this former 17th-century convent into a contemporary art center, more or less successfully marrying two styles of architecture. Happily they managed to preserve the old cloister. The bookshop has many books on design.

❾ Boadas★

Carrer Tallers, 1
☎ 93 318 88 26
Open Mon.-Sat. noon-2pm.

This copper and mahogany bar on the corner of the Ramblas is often frequented by politicians and intellectuals. It is reputed to have mixed the best cocktails in the city, *mojitos*, margaritas and dry martinis, since 1933. The founder, Boadas, learned the secrets of his trade in Havana, and the barman is of course a real expert.

❿ Casa Beethoven★★

Las Ramblas, 97
☎ 93 301 48 26
Open Mon.-Fri. 9am-8pm, Sat. 9am-1.30pm, 5-8pm.

Appropriately enough for its name, the owner is a pianist. The wooden shelves and the counter give off the sweetish smell of resin. For nearly a century the shop has been selling sheet music, catering for all genres from traditional *sardanas* to bossa nova, samba, rumba, Schubert and, of course, De Falla.

⓫ Xancò★

Las Ramblas, 78-80
☎ 93 318 09 89
Open Mon.-Fri. 10am-2pm, 4.30-8.30pm, Sat. 10am-2pm, 5-8.30pm.

Time has stood still at Xancò. Made-to-measure shirts have been produced here since 1820, adapting to changing fashions as the years have passed and all carefully arranged on carved wooden shelves. You can have your initials embroidered on the shirts and can choose from 29 colors in fine cotton poplin from around €60. The counter alone is worth the visit and you'll be able to see the superb oriental shop sign opposite B. Cuadros at no. 82.

⓬ Café de l'Òpera★

Las Ramblas, 74
☎ 93 302 41 80
Open Mon.-Thu. 9am-2.30pm, Fri. & Sat. 9am-3pm.

This bar opposite the Liceu theater was established in 1929 on the premises of a former chocolate shop, La Mallorquina, and is open and smoke-filled at all hours. The Thonet chairs and tarnished mirrors lend it a distinctive atmosphere. In the 1960s, it saw gatherings of Latin-American novelists, whose work was avidly consumed by the city. *Tertulias*, lengthy discussions on topic from jazz

:o medicine, were always in ‘ull swing. It’s popular with ›pera lovers as the Gran Teatre s across the road.

⓭ Herbolari Farran★★

›laça Reial, 18
☎ 93 304 20 05
Jpen Mon.-Sat.
›.30am-2pm, 4.30-8pm.

;o along pretty Bacardi ›assage to this first-rate ıerbalist. The fragrant plants ınd herbs exude health and

vell-being. You’ll find herbal eas to heal all ills, fragrant ›ssences and a surprisingly vide choice of so-called niracle cures.

⓮ Antiga Casa Figueras★★

Las Ramblas, 83
☎ 93 301 60 27
Open daily 8.30am-9pm.

The house of Escribà, the famous Catalan confectioners, has celebrated its 90th anniversary and smells as good as ever. Don’t miss the *pastas alimenticias* shop sign and the *Modernista* decor – sculpture, mosaics and stained-glass windows. All the applied arts on display here celebrate the art of good food.

LAS RAMBLAS

"Rambla" comes from the Arab word *ramla*, meaning sand. Las Ramblas follows the course of what was once a river. Until the 14th century it served as the western boundary of the city and marks the site of a 13th-century rampart, which allowed access to the city via the Santa Anna, Portaferissa, Boqueria and Drassana gates. Lamp posts along the *passeig* mark their former position. A mosaic of *azulejos* on Portaferissa street shows the layout of the old walls.

5

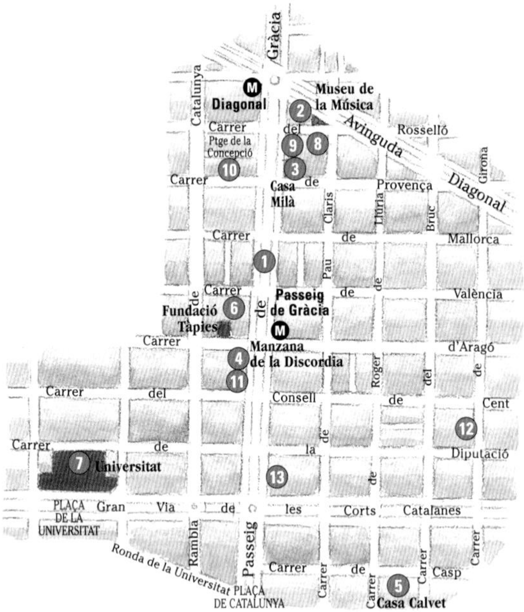

L'Eixample:
the marvels of Modernisme

At the turn of the 20th century the Eixample, literally "the extension," became the most prestigious part of the city. Many of its *Modernista* buildings house exclusive shops. The trendy lay siege to Vinçon to acquire the latest designer lamps, while swarms of tourists descend on Loewe and emerge triumphant, brandishing designer leather goods. Meanwhile, seated on benches in the wide avenues outside, businessmen pore over their the newspapers, one of the morning's ritual pleasures. It's an affluent and busy district, full of opulence.

❶ Passeig de Gràcia*

From 1890 to 1925, Passeig de Gràcia was an upper middle-class residential area. The city's first gas lamps were installed here and it became a fashionable place to walk at turn of the last century. The bourgoisie paraded in their horse-drawn carriages, their children accompanied by Galician nannies. Carnivals alternated with military processions, so there was frequently a festive air.

❷ Museu de la Música***

Avinguda Diagonal, 373
☎ 93 263 13 49
Open Tue.-Sun. 10am-2pm, Wed. 1-8pm.
Entry charge.

Known as the Palau Quadras, this building was erected by the architect Puig i Cadafalch in 1906. The beautiful staircase and mosaic floor,

columns with floral capitals and stone fountain of the entrance hall, all add up to a building of great harmony. The collection of musical instruments from the 16th to 20th century is particularly rich in guitars and there is an impressive display of organs.

❸ Casa Milà★★

Carrer Provença, 261-265
☎ 93 484 59 00
Rooms open Mon.-Sun. 10am-8pm.
Entry charge.

Gaudí's last, astonishing secular building was built between 1905 and 1910. Known locally as la Pedrera (the quarry), its undulating limestone façade – more sculpture than architecture –

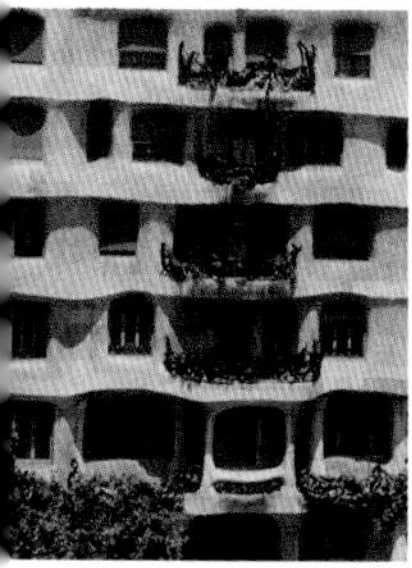

was to culminate in a tribute to the Virgin Mary, but his patrons, the Milà family, objected. Gaudí abandoned the project in order to devote his time and energy to La Sagrada Família (see p. 31). Casa Milà houses an attic exhibition space, a reconstruction of a *Modernista* flat, a gift and bookshop and, of course, the fabulous roof terrace with its strangely curving chimneys.

❹ Manzana de la Discordia★★★

Casa Lleò Morera (☎ 93 488 01 39, guided tours every hour Mon.-Sat. 10am-7pm, Sun.10am-2pm).
Casa Batllò (☎ 93 213 03 06 every day 10am-8pm)

Casa Amatller, (☎ 93 496 12 45, no tours but an information center on the *modernista* style is located on the ground floor)
Passeig de Gràcia.

At the turn of the last century each of the great families commissioned the most celebrated of the city's architects to erect suitably grand buildings in order to etch their names on posterity. The clashing styles of these buildings designed between 1898 and 1906 resulted in the name Manzana de la Discordia, or "Block of Discord." Architectural styles predating the industrial revolution were used as well as the *Modernista* style (see pp. 22-23). These lavish residences were designed and built on a strict rectangular grid plan, like pieces on a chess board, as you can see on the map.

❺ Casa Calvet★★

Carrer de Casp, 48
No tours.

This was Gaudí's first building, and the only one for which he was awarded a prize, in 1900. There are several strange things about it, including the three saints' heads provocatively watching passersby, richly decorated pulley supports and wrought-iron balustrade projections which soften and round off the rough stonework façade. It is now an apartment building.

❻ Fundació Antoni Tàpies★★★

Carrer d'Aragò, 255
☎ 93 487 03 15
Open Tue.-Sun. 10am-8pm.
Entry charge. (see p. 76)

This insitution is the result of the combined genius of two famous Catalan artists. In 1886 the architect Domenech i

Montaner designed the Montaner i Simon publishing house, which later became the Antoni Tàpies Foundation. The cast-iron and glass open-work exterior is ideal for exhibiting Tàpies' works (see p. 29). The building also houses a library and temporary exhibitions.

❼ Universitat★

Gran Via de les Corts Catalanes, 585. No tours.

The first university of Catalonia was founded at Lerida in 1300. At the start of the 15th century, King Martín the Humane introduced formalized teaching in the arts and medicine. The university had to move to Cervera in the 18th century, but the present neo-Romanesque building, by Elies Rogent, was not built until 1861. The library contains more than two million volumes, manuscripts and priceless early printed books.

❽ TincÇon★★

Carrer de Rosselló, 246
☎ 93 215 60 50
www.vincon.com
Open Mon.-Sat. 10am-2pm, 4.30-8.30pm.

TincÇon (a play on words meaning "I'm sleepy") is the little sister of the trendy shop Vinçon (see below) and sells everything you could think of to do with slumber, including sheets, pillowcases, bed linen

and even books on the subject. It also boasts the traditional high quality and innovative design found at Vinçon.

❾ Vinçon★★

Passeig de Gràcia, 96
☎ 93 215 60 50
www.vincon.com
Open Mon.-Sat. 10am-2pm, 4.30-8.30pm.

One day, a German by the name of Vinçon, decided to make his name in contemporary design. It was a wise decision as nowadays his shop stocks the best and most complete selection of design items for the home. You'll find everything here from the most avant-garde furniture to the latest gadgets for the bathroom, kitchen and office. The superb window displays have also become a showroom of contemporary design.

❿ Tragaluz★

Passatge de la Concepció, 5
☎ 93 487 06 21.
Open every day 1.30-4pm, 8.30pm-midnight (1am on Sat.).

This fashionable restaurant is a perfect example of its kind. The refined surroundings and quiet atmosphere offer a choice of stylish nouvelle cuisine dishes to match the setting, a turn-of-the-last-century villa with sophisticated decor. Choose a mezzanine table for the best view (around €24).

⓫ Antonio Miró★★

Carrer del Consell de Cent, 349
☎ 93 487 06 70
Open Mon.-Sat. 10am-8.30pm (closed in winter 12.30-4.30pm).

The Barcelona designer Antonio Miró is well regarded all over the world. The warm and graphic decor of his shop was designed by Pilar Lìbano in keeping with Miró's elegant line of clothes for both men and women. Women's suits cost from €420.

⓬ Le Café du Centre★★★

Carrer Girona, 69
☎ 93 488 11 01
Open Mon.-Fri. 7am-3am, Sat. 7.30pm-3am; in Feb. 10am-12.30pm, 4.30-8.30pm.

During the Republic (1931-1936), Le Café du Centre was a reputable and distinguished

gaming house. When gambling was prohibited, it was converted into a *bodega* serving a selection of cold ham and sausages, and *pa amb tomàquet*, slices of toasted bread with olive oil and tomatoes (€12). Ask for a table where L'Avi, a legendary croupier established his reputation.

⓭ Roca Jewelers★★

Passeig de Gràcia, 18
☎ 93 318 32 66
Open Mon.-Fri. 9.30am-1.30pm, 4.30-8pm, Sat. (in winter only) 10am-1.30pm, 5-8pm.

The interior of this jeweler's shop, the work of the architect Josep Lluis Sert, a friend of Joan Miró, is a superb example of rationalist architecture. Space, light and

color combine with the furniture to lend the decor great purity. The shop is the perfect setting for the jewelry and is definitely worth a visit.

THE CERDÀ PLAN

When the ramparts disappeared in 1854 the socialist engineer Idelfons Cerdà was given the task of drawing up plans for the Eixample (extension). Belonging to the generation of Proudhon, Hegel and the Romantic Movement he planned a modern, democratic city based on a grid shape cut diagonally by avenues. Work began in 1859 and an elegant and airy new district was born, with residential and apartment blocks, gardens and wide avenues.

6

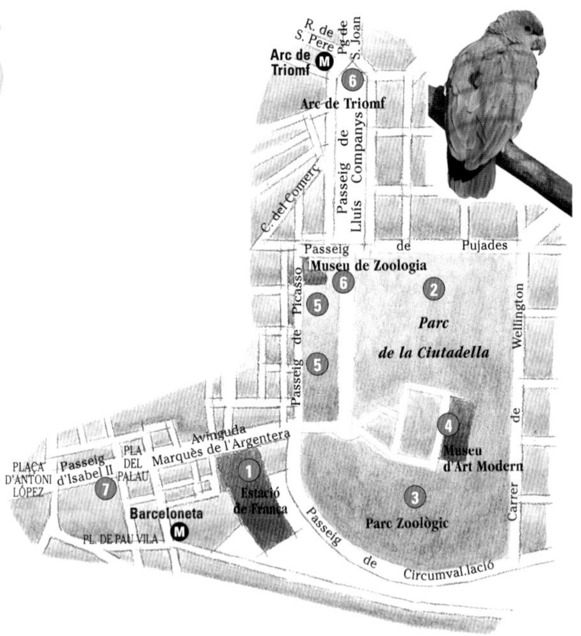

Ciutadella: a green haven

The Ciutadella park looks inviting enough for a stroll, and in summer provides an escape from the mugginess of the city. Lovers kiss on the boating lake while laughing children chase pigeons along the paths, ride their bicycles and greet the albino gorilla and zoo mascot. It's an open space filled with light that brightens up the dark, cramped maze of the old districts.

❶ Estació de França★★

Av. Marquès de l'Argentera
☎ 93 319 64 16
Open every day 6am-11.30pm.

The Estació de França station was built for the 1929 Universal Exhibition by the engineer A. Montaner, and restored in 1992. It was one of the most modern stations of its time, with metal arches spanning over 30m/100ft overhanging the platforms. Its splendid architecture can produce gasps even today.

❷ Parc de la Ciutadella★

Three entrances: Pg. Picasso, Pg. Pujades, C. Wellington.
Open every day 10am-5pm in winter, 9.30am-7.30pm in summer.

On September 11, 1714, the city surrendered to its new king, Philip V of Spain. A section of the Ribera district (see pp. 42-45) was razed to the ground in order to build a stronghold, symbolic of the subjugation of Barcelona by the Bourbons. The fortress was attacked in the 19th century during a resurgence of Catalan nationalism. It was demolished in 1868 and the area converted into a park.

❸ Parc Zoològic★

Parc de la Ciutadella
☎93 225 67 80
Open every day 10am-5pm in winter, 9.30am-7.30pm in summer.
Entry charge.

The Parc Zoològic occupies a good portion of the southeast part of the park. Colorful birds from all over the world – toucans, macaws and parrots, marmosets and dolphins, are all housed here, but the star exhibit is Copito de Nieve (Snowflake), the albino gorilla.

❹ Museu d'Art Modern de Catalunya★★★

Parc de la Ciutadella
☎93 319 57 28
Open every day except Mon. 10am-7pm Sun. 10am-2.30pm.
Entry charge.

Housed in the former arsenal, the museum presents a marvelous insight into turn-of-the-last-century Barcelona. The collections cover the period from 1830 to 1930. Look for Fortuny, Russinyol, Casas, Mir and Nonell. For *Modernista* and Noucentista architecture (see pp. 22-23), visit the room dedicated to the decorative arts, which reflects the interior of the buildings. Gaspar Homar's marquetry and the rippling lines of Gaudí chairs will delight the eye.

❺ Parc de la Ciutadella Umbracle and Hivernacle★★

☎93 295 40 17
Café Hivernacle open Mon.-Fri. 10am-midnight, Sat.-Sun. 10am-5pm.

This is an English-style park with two large glasshouses. One was called the Umbracle, built in 1883, a combination of ironwork columns and beams. It once housed a botanical school, but now contains teak deck chairs where you can lounge and dream of the tropics. The other, the Hivernacle, has a light ironwork structure, perfect for relaxing on a balmy summer evening.

❻ Arc de Triomf and Museu de Zoologia★★

Passeig Picasso
☎93 319 69 12
Open Tue.-Sun. 10am-2pm, Thu. 10am-6.30pm.
Entry charge.

The Parc de la Ciutadella staged the Universal Exhibition of 1888. The Arc de Triompf was erected as a monumental entrance, opening onto the Passeig San Joan. The former restaurant of the Exhibition now houses the Museu de Zoologia, which contains displays of stuffed animals and birds. Designed by Lluís Domenech i Montaner, the *Castell dels Tres Dragons* (Castle of the Three Dragons), as it came to be known, has medieval and Moorish elements.

❼ SET PORTES RESTAURANT★★

Passeig Isabel II, 14
☎93 319 30 33.
Open every day 1pm-1am.

An institution and cult venue with a visitors' book that has Che Guevara's signature alongside those of Manolete, John Wayne, Garcia Lorca, Miró and Ava Gardner. The 19th-century beams lit by rustic lamps are the ideal setting for a paella marinera or black rice from the Empordà (around €18).

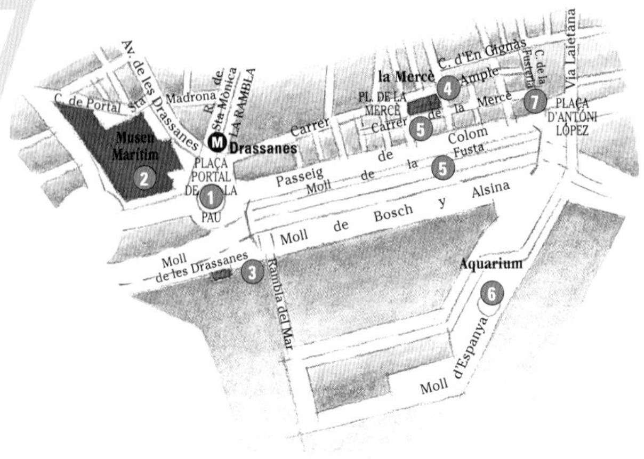

The port:
the call of the sea

People once used to approach Barcelona by boat and until 1900 visitors to the city landed by rowing boat. Nowadays, if you feel like seeing the port, you need to cross the elegant Rambla de Mar footbridge to the Moll d'Espanya. On Sundays, families come here to relax, proud to be part of this new capital of the Mediterranean which has, once more, resumed its vocation.

❶ Christopher Colombus Monument*

Plaça Portal de la Pau
☎ 93 302 52 24
Open 25 Sep.-30 Mar. Mon.-Fri. 10am-1.30pm, 3.30-6.30pm, Sat.-Sun. 10am-6.30pm; 1 Apr.-31 May, Mon.-Fri. 10am-2pm, 3.30-7.30pm, Sat.-Sun. 10am-7.30pm; 1 Jun.-24 Sep. every day 9am-8.30pm.
Entry charge.

The 50m/165ft-high column was erected for the Universal Exhibition of 1888, in homage to Christopher Columbus. From the top, you can pay your respects to the Genoese (or Catalan, as they say here) explorer at close range. His finger isn't pointing in the direction of America, but towards the Mediterranean, the source of the city's wealth.

❷ Drassanes and Museu Marítim**

Avinguda Drassanes
☎ 93 301 18 71
Open Mon.-Sun. 10am-7pm
Entry charge.

The ships built here from the 14th to 17th centuries were the largest in Europe. The industrial activity of the Drassanes, the medieval shipyards, was prolific producing commercial ships

to warships. At the Museu Marítim, you can discover more about this industry, admire the replica of the Royal galley that took part in the Battle of Lepanto (1571) and watch the film, "The Great Sea Adventure."

❸ Las Golondrinas, la Rambla de Mar*

Porta de la Pau
☎ 93 442 31 06
Departures every 35 minutes Mar.-Oct. every day 11am-8pm; Nov.-Feb. Sat.-Sun. 11am-4pm and weekday mornings.
Boarding charge.

To explore the port at water level, board a *golondrina*, a small boat moored by the quay. You'll be told the history of the harbor, whose first stone was laid in the 15th century. Since 1994, la Rambla de Mar, a swing footbridge in the form of a magnificent metal wave, has been outlined against the sky. It was designed by Viaplana and Pinon.

❹ Església de La Mercè and Carrer Ample*

Plaça de la Mercé
Open Mon.-Sat. 10am-1pm, 6-8.30pm, Sun. 10am-1.30pm, 7-8.30pm.

In the 18th century this district saw the building of the aristocratic residences on Carrer Ample. You'll have the best view of the Baroque façade of the basilica from the square with its imposing statue of Neptune. The church gained a reputation for buying back Catalan prisoners from the Barbary pirates. The Virgin of La Mercè, the city's venerated patron saint, is celebrated on 22nd and 24th September, with fireworks, parades of giants and *castellers* (see p. 16).

❺ Carrer de la Mercè and Moll de la Fusta*

Looking for a street with some *tapas*? There's **Pulperia** at 16 Carrer de la Mercè, with *patatas bravas* (a potato dish) and fried octopus to whet your appetite. **Bodega la Plata** at no. 28. serves local white wine from a *porrò* (see p. 11), accompanied by grilled sardines. If you prefer more trendy places, try the **Moll de la Fusta**, a promenade lined with bars and restaurants. One of the high notes is the sculpture by Roy Lichtenstein (1992), *La Cara de Barcelona* (*The Face of Barcelona*).

❻ Le Moll d'Espanya**

Maremagnum shopping centre:
Open every day 11am-11pm.
Aquarium:
(☎ 93 221 74 74
Open every day 9.30am-11pm (9pm in winter)
Entry charge.
Imax: (☎ 93 225 11 11
Entry charge.

This is the place to go if you're interested in the natural world. You can walk through the aquarium's 80m/260ft transparent tunnel and watch the dozen or so sharks at play, find out about the life of the beaver from the Imax cinema's 360-degree screen, buy organic cotton shirts from Peru at Natura and a toy for the children at Imaginarium (see p. 105).

❼ CERVANTÈS' HOUSE***

Passeig Colom, 2
No tours.
According to local tradition, no. 2 is nicknamed Casa Cervantès. Apparently the writer stayed here during a visit in 1610. The stone façade of the house can be distinguished by its ornate windows. Perhaps behind one of them Cervantès imagined *Don Quijote* on the beach of Barceloneta, fighting the White Moon knight.

8

From Barceloneta to Port Olímpic

Since 1992, the slogan *Barcelona oberta al mar* (Barcelona open to the sea) has become a fashionable theme. Town planners have transformed the coastline. Once you dined with your feet practically in the water in the *chiringuitos*, old family eateries that were abruptly torn down. If you're nostalgic for some Barceloneta "local color" then head for its central streets. You'll see washing fluttering on balconies, old people out for a breath of fresh air in their slippers, and cafés echoing to cheers as Barça score another goal.

❶ Marina Port Vell★★

The city hasn't always benefited from the sheltered port it has today. Until the 19th century ships had to stay out at sea while small craft transferred their merchandise to the shore. Port Vell is the old port, whose main feature today is the Maremagnum leisure complex of shops and bars. The marina is an addition from 1992, and the yachts add a touch of luxury to one of the oldest industrial parts of the port.

2 Palau de Mar, Museu d'Història Catalunya★★★

Plaça Pau Vila
☎ 93 225 47 00
Open Tue.-Sat. 10am-7pm (8pm on Wed.), Sun. 10am-2.30pm
Entry charge.

The Palau de Mar, part of the 19th-century docks, is an old warehouse. which has been given a face-lift, but remains a fine example of industrial architecture. These "general warehouses for trade and commerce" house the new Museum of Catalan History,

spread over two floors. Great moments in Catalan history are presented in an educational and entertaining way, through displays, films, special effects, interactive screens and hands-on exhibits. Afterwards, you can enjoy something to eat on the terrace of the docks and dream of pirates and buccaneers.

3 Moll dels Pescadors★★

Cable-car open every day 11am-7pm (in good weather).
Entry charge.

The fishermen's jetty is only accessible during the fish auctions, when the place becomes a hive of activity from

daybreak onward as the fish wholesalers bid for the best parts of the catch. At night the jetty is lit by the glow from the light of the old beacon (1772). St. Sebastiàn's Tower is a familiar sight in the port and forms the terminus for the cable-car, which you can take back to Monjuïc.

4 Barceloneta and its beach★★

Barceloneta is home to part of the city's folklore. It was

created in the 18th century, when the Ribera (see pp. 42-45) was razed to the ground to build the Ciutadella (see pp. 56-57). Its inhabitants had to wait until 1753 to be rehoused in Barceloneta. It has retained the charm of some of the old Mediterranean cities – you could easily be in Palermo or Naples. The people of Barcelona bathed at the Banos St. Sebastiàn and the Banos Orientales at the turn of the last century. Today, however, it is the city's best loved playground and there's a 5km/3 mile stretch of palm-fringed beach popular with bathers and sun-worshipers alike.

5 Església de Sant Miquel del Port★

Open every day 7am-1.45pm, 4.30-8pm.

This church was built when Barceloneta was in its infancy, in 1753, in honor of St Miquel, Barceloneta's patron saint. Its façade is a fine example of Baroque architecture. In summer, it's delightfully cool and children play football outside in the square to cries of "Força Barça."

❻ Passeig Marítim, water tower and gasometer*

Passeig Marítim links 18th-century Barceloneta with Port Olímpic. As you walk along it, you'll discover what remains of the area's industrial past. The *Modernista* silhouette of the water tower by J. Domenech i Estapà, built in 1906, is very striking and the old metal structure of the former gasometer will soon become the centerpiece of a park.

❼ Port Olímpic and *Whale* by Frank Gehry**

The designer restaurants of Port Olímpic have replaced the cheaper, unassuming restaurants which lined the shore just a few years ago. It's quite usual to see several generations gather round a table for a family meal on Sunday. Grab an ice-cream or some *pipas* (roasted sunflower seeds) and take a stroll along the quays in the afternoon. A vast bronze whale is 'beached' here. Its 50m/165ft skeleton was designed by the architect Frank Gehry. In 1992 during the Barcelona Olympic Games, the watersport events were started from here.

❽ Arts Hotel*

Carrer de la Marina 19-21
☎93 221 10 00.

Two towers dominate Port Olímpic. One of them, designed by Ortiz i Leon, houses Mapfre Insurance; the second is the luxurious Arts-Ritz-Carlton hotel. Its Terraza bar (open every day 7am-2am) has one of the best views of Frank Gehry's whale, not to mention an overview of the port itself. The hotel's choice of *puros* (cigars) and *cavas* (local champagne) cocktails is excellent. For "designer *tapas*" try **Goyescas**, the hotel restaurant (open Mon.-Fri. 1-10pm, Sat. evenings only, closed Sun.).

❾ Nova Icària*

Nova Icària is the latest redevelopment project for 130 ha/320 acres of coastline. It has appropriated part of the Poble Nou, the "Catalan Manchester" of the 19th century, where only a few factory chimneys remain as a reminder of the area's industrial past. In the 1990s, architects backed by property developers created the city of the future – the Olympic Village, where athletes were

housed during the 1992 Olympic Games. Manuel Vázquez Montalbán, the writer, wrote:

"The new Olympic Village is like an Oxford graduate playing cricket at the doors of the Bronx."

⑩ Baja Beach Club★★★

Passeig Marítim
☎93 225 91 00
Restaurant open every day 1pm-5am.

One of the most popular of the new bars which go in and out of fashion so quickly, the Beach Club is the latest trendy venue, a disco, café and restaurant all rolled into one. It features vulgar shows and sexy waitresses, so be warned! The menu is American-style, but people really come here more for the entertainment than for the food.

⑪ Two open-air sculptures★★★

The streets and squares of Barcelona include over 430 monuments. Many of them were erected during the first 30 years of the 20th century, but their number multiplied in the 1980s and 1990s. One example from what you might term this open-air museum is Antoni Llena's *David and Goliath* (1993). Another is by Rebecca Horn. Her sculpture *Hommage to Barceloneta* (1992) is on the beach. It evokes the *chiringuitos* (see panel below), the little kiosks selling food which have since vanished.

⑫ L'Antiga Casa Solé★★

Carrer Sant Carlos, 4
☎ 93 221 50 12
Open Tue.-Sun. 1-4pm, 8.30-11pm.

This port *bistrot*, which opened in 1903, still has four of its original marble tables, its waiters still wear white jackets and the beer is still draft. The open-plan kitchen is clearly visible to the diners, who can see the delicious dishes being prepared in front of them. *Sarsuela* (Catalan fish stew) was invented here and Casa Solé has been serving delicious traditional dishes ever since.

LOS CHIRINGUITOS

From 1941 onwards, fishermen's families traditionally prepared simple meals and snacks for bathers on the beach at Barceloneta, cooked in *chiringuitos*, little kiosks. These kiosks proliferated in the San Sebastiàn and Los Orientales areas, and were only open in summer. However, in 1991, the kiosks were sadly demolished, and part of the city's folklore and history disappeared along with them.

9

Diagonal Pedralbes: the city heights

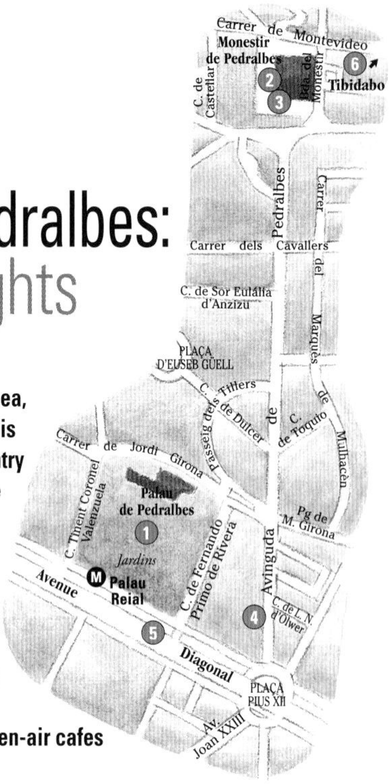

Mountains and plains, sky and sea, Pyrenees and Mediterranean, this duality defines the Catalan country and its capital. For centuries the lure of a vista across the countryside or over the sea has drawn the people of Barcelona to its heights. Monasteries, villas, gardens and parks are dotted around the hillsides. In summer the light breezes are heaven-sent and open-air cafes are much in demand.

❶ Jardíns and Palau de Pedralbes★★

Avinguda Diagonal, 686
Museu de les Arts Decoratives
☎ 93 280 50 24
Museu de Ceràmica
☎ 93 280 16 21
Open Tue.-Sat. 10am-6pm, Sun. 10am-3pm.
Joint ticket.

This royal residence was built in the 1920s on land that once belonged to Don Güell. It houses the Museu de les Arts Decoratives and Museu de Ceràmica, with unique pieces with enamel decoration by Artigas, Miró and Picasso.

❷ Monestir de Pedralbes★★

Baixada Monestir, 9
☎ 93 203 92 82
Open Tue.-Sun. 10am-2pm.
Entry charge.

This is one of the most attractive places to take a walk in the city. The name Pedralbes probably comes from the Latin *petras albas* (white stone). Commissioned around 650 years ago by Elisende de Montcada, wife of Jaume II, the church was consecrated in 1327. On her husband's death the queen retreated to the monastery surrounded by her court. The three-story cloisters evoke some 600 years of convent life, and are a fine illustration of Catalan Gothic architecture. In St. Michael's chapel, the murals of Ferrer Bassa are

evidence of the close ties between the Italians and Catalans in the 14th century.

❸ Col.lecció Thyssen-Bornemisza★★★

Baixada Monestir, 9
☎ 93 280 14 34
Open Tue.-Sun. 10am-2pm.
Entry charge.

Since 1993, the Monastery of Pedralbes has exhibited part of the Thyssen-Bornemisza Collection. Former dormitories of the St. Clare of Assisi order of nuns were converted to house the art collection, more evidence of the close links between medieval Italy and Catalonia. It features 13th- to 18th-century paintings from European Schools. If you're short of time, the highlights are Fra Angelico's *Virgin of Humility*, Titian's *Virgin and Child*, Tintoretto's *Portrait of the Senator*, Ruysdaël's *Seascape*, Canaletto's *Bucentaure* and Guardi's *St. Mark's Square*.

❹ Entrance to the Finca Güell★★

Avinguda Pedralbes, 7.

The main gate and entrance pavilions of the Finca Güell by Gaudí once again demonstrate his tireless ornamental inventiveness. The Moorish caretaker's lodge could be mistaken for a sultan's harem, and the dragon standing guard is undoubtedly a Catalan Art-Nouveau wrought-iron masterpiece, with menacing jaws.

❺ Avinguda Diagonal★

This avenue crosses the city from east to west and was planned in 1859, like **L'Eixample** (see pp. 52-55). At the top is the business center, with luxury hotels, insurance companies, large department stores (Illa and Corte Inglès, see pp. 106-107) and banks. The façade of the Caixa de Pensions displays a logo designed by Miró. This five-pointed star is the emblem of one of the most powerful banking organizations in Europe.

❻ THE ASCENT OF TIBIDABO★★★

If you'd like to see some views, take a taxi to the foot of the Tibidabo mountain (10 minutes from Pedralbes). Then take the *tramvía blau*, one of the last vestiges of Barcelona's tram system. This "electric" ascent to the summit gives you the opportunity to admire the *Modernista* villas built by the Barcelona middle classes at the turn of the last century. Every respectable family had a *torre* (villa) in the countryside. At the end of the journey, take a rest on the terrace of **La Venta** (see p. 92).

10

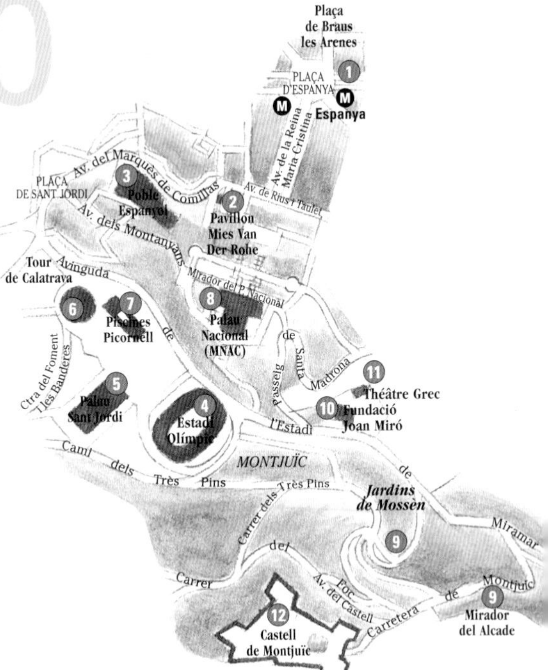

Montjuïc: the reclaimed hill

Montjuïc was named after the Jewish community that once lived here. Given a costly face-lift for the 1992 Olympic Games, the people of Barcelona now mainly come for the fresh air, though there's a lot to do and see. You can have a picnic, stroll along the terraces of the Miró Foundation, place a bet at the Plaça d'Espanya greyhound track, or, if you really must, go for a jog – the marathon entrance to the Olympic stadium isn't far away.

❶ Carrer de Llancà and Plaça de Braus les Arenes★★

Open Mon., Fri.-Sun. 11am-2pm, 5-9pm, Tue.-Thu. 5-9pm Free entry.

The Plaça d'Espanya, at the site of a former crossroads, was built for the 1929 Universal Exhibition (see p. 69). At its center is an ornate fountain by J.M. Jujol, a colleague of Gaudí, which represents the rivers of the Iberian Peninsula. To the north lies the "neo-Moorish" bullring of 1899 which is no longer in use as the Catalans despise the bull-fighting lifestyle of Madrid.

❷ Pavelló Mies Van der Rohe★★

Av. del Marquès de Comillas

☎ 93 423 40 16
Open every day 10am-8pm.
Entry charge.

The Pavelló Mies Van Der Rohe lies at the foot of the Montjuïc. It was destroyed at the end of the 1929 Universal Exhibition, but then was reconstructed in 1986. It has a simple, abstract shape, made of marble, stone, onyx and glass.

❸ Poble Espanyol*

Av. del Marquès de Comillas
☎ 93 325 78 66
Open Mon. 9am-6pm, Tue.-Thu. 9am-2pm, Fri.-Sat. 9am-4pm, Sun. 9am-6pm.
Entry charge.

This "Spanish Village" was initially conceived for visitors to the 1929 Universal Exhibition as a lightning tour of Spain, but is still just as popular today, representing as it does the diversity of Spanish regional architecture. Folk crafts, such as ceramics, are on sale in the village and there are restaurants serving regional dishes. Climb to the top of the Torres de Avila to the bar of the same name (see p. 132) for a fine view.

❹ Estadi Olímpic and Galería*

Av. de l'Estadi
Stadium open every day 10am-6pm (8pm in summer).
Entry free at Puerta Maraton. Galería (☎ 93 426 06 60)
Open Apr.-Sep. Mon.-Fri. 10am-2pm, 4-7pm; Oct.-Mar. Mon.-Fri. 10am-1pm, 4-6pm.
Entry charge at South Gate.

The walls by Pere Domenech date from 1929, and the façade and equestrian sculptures by Gargallo have also been preserved. You can just imagine some 60,000 spectators in full voice cheering the athletes on to victory. In the gallery you can see the costumes created by Els Comedians for the Olympic ceremonies.

❺ Palau Sant Jordi***

Av. de l'Estadi
☎ 93 426 20 89
Open every day 10am-8pm.
Free entry to the Olympic Esplanade.

The Japanese architect Arata Isozaki made use of state-of-the-art technology when designing the site of the 1992 Olympic gymnastics events. However, nowadays the athletes have been supplanted by showbiz, and rock concerts now call the tune. At sunset, Miyawaki's sculptures create a beautiful graphic effect – a forest of metallic trees, futuristic creations, are outlined against the sky.

❻ Calatrava tower**

Plaça Europa
Free entry.

This space-age telecommunications tower is the elegant counterpoint of the Palau Sant Jordi. It was designed by Santiago Calatrava and dominates the skyline, pointing the way to new horizons.

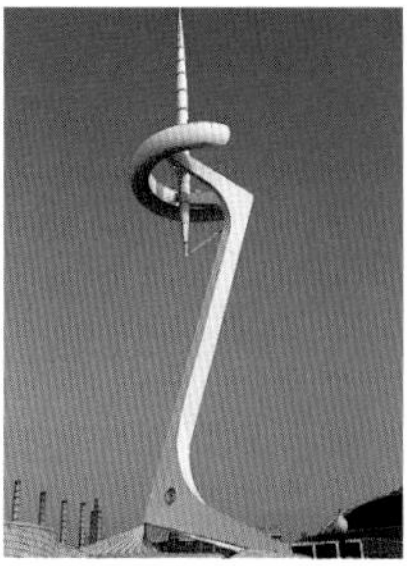

❼ Picornell swimming pools and INEFC★

Avinguda de l'Estadi.

The swimming-pool complex was remodeled for the Olympics and is named after Bernat Picornell, the Catalan swimming pioneer. It rubs shoulders with the neo-Classical building of the Institut Nacional de Educació Fisica de Catalunya (INEFC). The latter, built round a cloister, is typical of its Catalan designer, Ricardo Bofill. The entrance is a portico with

Doric columns, like an ancient Greek temple. The light-colored building stands out against a radiant blue sky, once again to grandiose effect.

❽ Museu Nacional d'Art de Catalunya (MNAC)★★

Parc Montjuïc
☎ 93 622 03 76
Open Tue.-Sat. 10am-7pm, Sun. & public hols 10am-2.30pm.
Entry charge.

Symbol of the 1929 Exhibition and restored by Gae Aulenti, the former National Palace has housed collections of Catalan art since 1934. Don't miss the superb Roman and Gothic collections. There are remarkable 12th-century frescoes by Urgell and Taüll.

This, the best of the art museums in Barcelona, is being renovated and reorganized and the collection from the Museu d'Art Modern in Cuitadella park was moved here too.

❾ Mirador de l'Alcalde and Mossen Gardens Costa i Llobrera

Plaça del Mirador
Free entry.

Opposite the entrance to the amusement park and esplanade, this provides one of the most enjoyable views of the port. The pavement is a collage of ceramic fragments and bottle bases. A sculpture by

Subirachs pays "Homage to Barcelona." Down below, the Mossen Gardens go cascading down to the port.

❿ Fundació Joan Miró★★★

Parc Montjuïc
☎ 93 329 19 08
Open Tue.-Sat. 10am-7pm (8pm Jul.-Sep.), Sun. 10am-2.30pm.
Entry charge.

This beautiful white building housing the works of Joan Miró was opened in 1975. Designed by his friend Josep Lluis Sert, it lies in a magical setting in the gardens overlooking the city. The works – paintings, sculptures, tapestries and graphics – cover the period 1914 to 1978 and were donated by Miró himself.

There is a restaurant and bookshop.

⓫ Teatre Grec*

Passeig de l'Exposició.

This reproduction Greek theater was installed in a disused quarry below the Miró Foundation for the 1929 Exhibition. The quarry's sandstone has been used to build the city since Roman times. In the Middle Ages porters carried the stone down from Montjuïc for the building of Santa Maria del Mar free of charge. The theater is now used during the city's cultural festival held in summer. If you can get tickets, an evening watching a performance here as the sun sets is just magical.

⓬ Castell de Montjuïc and Military Museum

Summit of Montjuïc Hill
☎ 93 329 86 13
Open Tue.-Sun. 9.30am-8pm (summer), 9.30am-4.30pm (winter).
Entry charge.

The castle of Montjuïc has witnessed some bloody times. Designed in 1751 in the shape of a star by the engineer Cermeno, it was from here that the city was bombarded in the

1942 rebellion, and five prisoners were executed here by firing squad in 1896. It has housed the Museu Militar (military history museum) since 1960 and displays fine collections of weaponry, armor, uniforms and maps, as well as portraits of the counts and kings of Catalonia.

MONTJUÏC, SITE OF THE 1929 EXHIBITION

In May 1929, Alphonse XIII inaugurated the Universal Exhibition. It was a showcase for the dictatorship of Primo de Rivera, and only survived him by a few weeks. Most of the buildings you'll see on the hillsides are former pavilions that have been turned into museums or theaters. The Mercat dels Flors theater, for example, is a strange and ghostly place, but worth a detour.

11

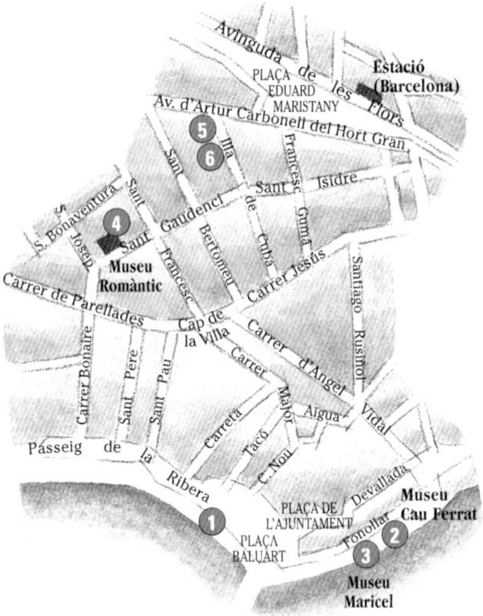

Sitges:
a short hop to the beach

The sandy beaches of the Costa Daurada lie between Barcelona and Tarragona. Sitges has been spared by developers and retains the elegant character of a turn-of-the-last-century holiday resort, with several *Modernista* villas, a palm-fringed *passeig* (promenade), and a church with a pink façade. The resort is perhaps best known for its pulsating nightlife and is also a popular gay holiday destination.

❶ Church square and Passeig de la Ribera★★★

The origins of this once sleepy fishing port are steeped in history. It is said to have been an ancient site and the maritime outlet for the mountain city of Oderdola. The name Sitges is of Iberian origin and means "silos," and it is certainly true that stocks of grain have been discovered in hollows carved out of the rock. From the 17th-century church square you can see the promenade which runs the length of the Platja d'Or.

❷ Museu Cau Ferrat★★

Carrer Fonollar,
☎ 93 894 03 64

Open in winter: Tue.-Fri. 10am-1.30pm, 3-6.30pm, Sat. 10am-7pm, Sun. 10am-3pm; in summer: Tue.-Sun. 10am-2pm, 5-9pm.
Joint ticket for the three museums (2, 3 and 4).

In 1893, the artist and writer Santiago Rusiñol acquired a fisherman's cottage and set up his studio here. His collections of wrought-iron work, ceramics and Catalan furniture were bequeathed to the city by his widow. See the two works by El Greco that Rusiñol paraded through the streets to parody the Easter procession, and paintings by Picasso, Ramon Casas and Nonell.

❸ Museu Maricel★

For details see Museu Cau Ferrat.

The former city hospital houses valuable Spanish works

of art donated by a collector. The Gothic rooms contain altar-pieces with gold backgrounds and multi-colored carved wooden sculptures. The entrance hall decorated by Josep Maria Sert (1874-1945), painter of theatrical frescoes and the husband of Mysia, the muse of the Ballets Russes, is quite a curiosity. On the top floor the Roig collection contains displays of model ships and musical instruments.

❹ Museu Romàntic★

Carrer San Gaudenci, 1
☎ 93 894 29 69
For details see Museu Cau Ferrat.

This former residence of the Llopis family dates from 1793.

The furniture of the period has been preserved, as have the murals by Pau Rigalt tracing the life of the city in the late 18th century. It shows the life of a bourgois family in the 18th and 19th centuries. There is also a collection of delicate old dolls, with pretty hats, little bags, muffs and parasols.

❺❻ El Xalet Hotel-Restaurant★★

Carrer Isla de Cuba, 35
☎ 93 811 00 70
Open May.-Oct. every day 8-11.30pm.

The architect Buigas built this *Modernista* villa in the 19th century. When the *Indianos* – residents who had made their fortune abroad at the end of the 19th century – returned to the country, they wanted to build luxurious residences. Sitges has a good number of these mansions. Entering the dining room of the El Xalet is like stepping back in time. You feel as if you should be taking part in a period film. Try some of the delicious home cooking prepared by the proprietor (around €24). A double room costs in the region of €54.

SANTIAGO RUSIÑOL (1861-1931)

Born of a middle-class family that had made its fortune during the industrial revolution, Rusiñol preferred the Bohemian lifestyle to that of his own class. A fervent Catalan, he traveled abroad regularly and during his stays in Paris cultivated friendships with the painters of Montmartre. He also helped many artists from Barcelona to become known. From 1892 to 1899, Rusiñol organized the Festes Modernistes, artistic gatherings of music, painting, sculpture and dance and Sitges became a Mecca del Modernismo, or Mecca of Modernism.

The Town's History Museum

In 1931, the Gothic palace of the Casa Clarina-Padellàs was moved from the Carrer dels Mercaders to the Plaça del Rei, stone by stone, to house the History Museum. A visit to the museum will take you through 2,000 years of the city's history, as you walk through the ancient Barcino (which later became Barcelona) and discover multiple aspects of its everyday life, thanks to the numerous excavated artifacts on display and a series of striking reconstructions.

Barcino: the Barcelona of Roman times

As an introduction, you will learn about the Iberic people who occupied the plain of Barcelona before the arrival of the Romans. Next, you will discover Barcino, the ancient Barcelona, a fortified Roman town which covered 10ha (25 acres). Remains of its public monuments, such as the columns of a 1st-century BC temple and the towers and fortified walls from the 4th century AD, are still visible in the Barrio Gótico district.

The archeological complex

Spreading under the actual city, over a surface of 3,716sq m (40,000sq ft), this archeological complex is one of the largest underground museums in Europe.

You will first be taken along the Roman wall, following the *intervallum*, a street which circled the whole city from the outside and helped defend it. You will then enter the craftsmen's district, where you can visit a 2nd-century workshop, dedicated to the washing and dyeing of cloth, and a 3rd-century fishery. Finally, you will discover an Episcopal complex, built between the 5th and the 7th centuries, composed of a palace, a baptistery and the bishop's reception hall, decorated with wall paintings.

INFORMATION

Town's History Museum
(see pp. 40-41)
Metro Jaume I
☎ 93 315 11 11
Open Tue.-Sat. 10am-2pm, 4-8pm, Sun. 10am-2pm
Entrance charge.

The Picasso Museum

The Picasso Museum occupies five medieval mansions in the Ribera district: the palace of Berenguer d'Aguilar, the Baró de Castellet palace, the Baroque Mecca palace, the Casa Mauri and Palau Finestres. The museum's collection is composed of 3,000 works, most of which were donated by Jaime Sabartès, the secretary of Pablo Picasso, and a personal friend. In 1968, works from Picasso's youth, which had remained in the hands of his Catalan family, were added to the collection. The exceptional wealth of its collection make it the most visited museum in Barcelona.

The early years

A visit to the museum begins with drawings that Picasso executed when he was only nine years old, and notably by a striking *Self-portrait* in charcoal. Caricatures he did of his teachers in the margins of his schoolbooks are also on view. The *First Communion* (1895-1896) was presented by Picasso at the Barcelona Decorative Arts Exhibition. As for *Science and Charity* (1897), a huge and forceful oil painting in which his father plays the part of a doctor, it earned him a prize from the Arts Academy of Barcelona.

Masterpieces

One of the museum's rooms is dedicated to the 44 paintings Picasso executed between August 17 and December 30 of 1957, all of which were inspired by one of Velásquez's great paintings, *Las Meninas* (*The Maids of Honor*), depicting the women of the Spanish court. Also on view are the preparatory sketches Picasso made in 1937 for his famous *Guernica*.

Ceramics

The ceramics collection is composed of 41 boldly painted pieces, donated by Jacqueline Picasso, the artist's wife, in 1982. Made between 1947 and 1965, they offer precious insight into the painter's artistic and technical evolution.

INFORMATION

Picasso Museum (see p. 40) C. Montcada, 15-19 Metro Jaume I
☎ 93 319 63 10
Tue.-Sat. 10am-8pm and Sun. 10am-3pm
Bookshop and restaurant
Entrance charge.

Museum of Contemporary Art

The MACBA has become a reference in the city's artistic and cultural life, offering visitors the chance to discover contemporary art in the best possible conditions. Inaugurated on November 29, 1995, it gives a chronological presentation of Catalan, Spanish and foreign artists' work from the second half of the 20th century.

The building
The MACBA's design, by American architect Richard Meir, was part of a vast urban renovation project of the Raval district. This magnificent building, which looks like a single white block cut in straight lines and curves, also has large openings whose purpose is to let the daylight inside the museum.

Temporary exhibitions
Much of the museum's space is given over to temporary exhibitions that focus on contemporary social issues, such as the role of artistic creation and the artist's responsibility. This thematic approach sheds new light over artists' works by placing them in different contexts, and encouraging multiple interpretations.

The permanent exhibition
The collection is organized in three main periods. The first extends from the 1940s to the 1960s, and focuses on the artistic movement which followed the surrealist revolution. The second period, which covers the 1960s and th 1970s, hinges on the events of May 1968. Those two decades saw the emergence of new modes of expression, stemming from artists' eagerness to rethink art as a whole.

Finally, the works of Penck, Zush and Carlos Pazos illustrate the influence of new technologies on artists' work from the 1980s to this day.

INFORMATION
Museum of Contemporary Art
(see p. 47)
Pl. dels Àngels, 1
Metro Catalunya
☎ 93 412 08 10
Open Mon., Wed.-Fri. 11am-8pm (in winter until 7.30pm),
Sat. 11am-8pm,
Sun. 10am-1pm
Entrance charge.

The Catalan National Museum of Art

The National Palace of Montjuïc, built for the 1929 Barcelona International Exhibition, has housed the Catalan National Museum of Art (MNAC) since 1934. The contents of its extraordinary collection of Gothic and Romanesque art originate mainly from the small churches of Catalonia and Aragon.

Romanesque art

Displayed in their original contexts, thanks to exceptional reconstructions of apses, crypts, vaults and chapels, the museum has the world's greatest collection of Romanesque frescoes. Also of particular interest are the wooden sculptures, the retables painted in splendid colors, and the liturgical objects in bronze and copper.

Gothic art

The collection of Gothic paintings and sculptures is just as impressive. It contains masterpieces from all over Spain, among which are the Gothic retables of Jaume Huguet, *St. George and the Princess*, originally meant for the churches of Sant Agustí Vell and Santa Maria del Pi, the paintings of Bernat Martorell and *The Virgin of the Counsellors* by Lluís Dalmau. The sheer quantity of works, while displaying a marvelous diversity of styles, also helps illustrate the evolution of sculpture and painting over this period.

Medieval Barcelona

A number of Gothic and Romanesque masterpieces originate from Barcelona's own religious sanctuaries. These include the decorative sculptures of the old Romanesque Cathedral, from the 11th century, the capitals from the columns of Sant Pere de les Puelles and the sculptures from the convents del Carme and Sant Francesc.

INFORMATION

Catalan National Museum of Art (see p. 68).
Parc Montjuïc
Metro Catalunya
☎ 93 622 03 76
Open Tue.-Sat. 10am-7pm, Sun. and feasts 10am-2.30pm.
Entrance charge.

The Tàpies Foundation

In order to promote a better understanding of the art and culture of the last century, and to encourage their study, Catalan artist Antoni Tàpies created the foundation, which bears his name, in 1984. Most of the works of the collection were donated by Teresa and Antoni Tàpies.

The building

Between 1880 and 1885, the architect Lluís Domènech i Montaner (1849-1923) erected a building in the Eixample district, commissioned by the Editorial Montaner i Simón publishing house. One century later, the building was refitted by architects Roser Amadó and Lluís Domènech Girbau, in order to house the Antoni Tàpies collection. The edifice was built using a variety of materials. Its structure is made of steel and glass and its façade covered in bricks. Large rose windows and the sculpted busts of famous writers decorate the exterior of the building. On its roof sits a large aluminum tube sculpture, named *Cloud and Chair,* executed by Tàpies in 1990.

The collection

The works exhibited in this museum span Antoni Tàpies' whole artistic career. They show how the artist perfected certain techniques (such as gluing, scratching and assemblage) and explain his interest for recycling and the use of rough materials, such as rope and paper. As for his taste for vivid colors, this is perfectly illustrated by the work named *Lithography*, from 1948, in which he used the colors of the Catalan flag.

The research center

Thanks to numerous events (temporary exhibitions, of both modern and contemporary art, conferences, etc.), the foundation has established its reputation as a dynamic research center. Its library contains a large number of documents on 20th-century art and Asian culture.

INFORMATION

Tàpies Foundation
(see pp. 53-54)
Carrer d'Aragó, 255
Metro Passeig de Gràcia
☎ 93 487 03 15
Open Tue.-Sun.
10am-8pm
Entrance charge.

The Thyssen-Bornemisza Collection

The Thyssen-Bornemisza Collection is composed of Italian, Flemish, German, Dutch, Spanish and French works of art from the 13th to the 20th centuries. They were brought together by Baron Heinrich Thyssen-Bornemisza and his son Hans Heinrich. This exceptional collection was divided in 1992 between a Madrid museum and the Barcelona Foundation. It contains works by the greatest masters of European painting: Fra Angelico, Veronese, Zurbaran, Velásquez, Rubens, Tiepolo…

The Pedralbes Monastery

In 1326, Queen Elisenda de Montcada (1293-1364) founded the Pedralbes monastery for the sisters of the order of Saint Clare. The ancient dormitory and reception hall located on the first floor of the building were restored to accommodate the 72 paintings and eight sculptures of the foundation. Of particular interest in this magnificent example of Gothic Catalan architecture, are the 15th-century windows and the vault's lancet arches, only partly hidden by a 16th-century wooden ceiling.

Medieval Art

Among the eight sculptures and 17 paintings from the Italian Renaissance, Fra Angelico's *Virgin of Humility* (1433-1435) and Titian's influential *Virgin and Child* deserve particular attention.

Venetian late Baroque

Paintings of religious themes and urban scenes reveal the extraordinary vitality of 18th-century Venice, one of the most important cultural and commercial centers of the Mediterranean. Canaletto's *The Bucentaure* (1745-1750) illustrates the city's expansive ambitions. The doge, having embarked on *the Bucentaure*, heads out for the Laguna, escorted by richly decorated gondolas, to seal an alliance with the sea, with the symbolical gift of a golden ring.

INFORMATION

Thyssen-Bornemisza Foundation (see p. 65)
Baixada Monestir, 9
☎ 93 280 14 34
Open Tue.-Sun.
10am-2pm
Entrance charge.

The Joan Miró Foundation

In 1971, Joan Miró decided to create a space dedicated to the study and promotion of his work and of contemporary art. The Modern Art Center of the Miró Foundation was opened to the public on June 10, 1975. With more than one thousand drawings, paintings, ceramics, tapestries, theater sets, sculptures and photographs, it constitutes the world's largest and most comprehensive collection of the artist's works.

The building

To house the collection, the architect Lluís Sert created a modern building, remarkable for the purity of its design. Its exceptionally luminous interiors enhance the works of Miró and of the other artists whose works are on display (Calder, Ernst, Duchamp and Matisse).

The collection

The bulk of the collection was donated by Joan Miró, even if a certain number of works originate from the collections of Joan Prats and Pilar Juncosa, the artist's wife. Of particular interest are the *Painting after a Collage* (1933), making use of a technique which was to become a hallmark of the artist's work, a surprising *Self-portrait* (1937-1960) – thick black lines and five blobs of color are superimposed over a lead-pencil drawing – and *The Hope of the Condemned Man*, a triptych in which a single black line first evokes a human profile and then fades away, along with the life and hopes of the condemned man.

Outside the museum

The gardens and the large terrace of the Miró Foundation deserve a visit, for they are not only home to the artist's sculptures, but also offer a splendid view over Barcelona.

The research center

The Foundation holds numerous archives and over 19,000 documents. The contemporary art bookshop offers catalogs, brochures, posters and highly amusing mementoes.

INFORMATION

Joan Miró Foundation
(see pp. 68-69)
Parc Montjuïc
Metro Poble Sec, Espanya or funicular Paral.lel
☎ 93 329 19 08
Open Tue.-Sat. 10am-7pm (Thu. to 9.30pm, Jul.-Sep. to 8pm), Sun. 10am-2.30pm
Entrance charge.

The Sagrada Família

The Sagrada Família is both the symbol of Barcelona and Antoni Gaudí's most famous achievement. Living like a recluse inside the building for more than 16 years, Gaudí devoted his life to this project, but he did not live to see its completion. After the accident that cost him his life in 1926, he was buried in the crypt.

An ambitious project

When Gaudí took over the neo-gothic project started by Francesc de Villar in 1883, he was intent on building a "cathedral for the 20th century" which would take its inspiration from nature. The building, featuring five naves and spectacular vertical dimensions, was to boast monumental façades representing the birth, death and resurrection of Christ. Towers covered in mosaic-work would symbolize the 12 apostles, the four evangelists, the Virgin and Christ.

Unfinished work

The construction of the cathedral is still far from complete. Of Antoni Gaudí's initial projects, only a few elements have actually been finished. These include the Nativity façade, the cathedral's highlight, on the east side with its astounding decorative work (moldings of flora and fauna, statues, carved stone friezes); and the façade of the Passion (west side) with its four towers built between 1954 and 1976.

Visits

There are still works being carried out across much of the site. However, in the parts that are open to the public, don't miss the crypt, completed in 1882 by Francesc de Villar, the neo-gothic apse and the altar canopy, both by Antoni Gaudí. If you are feeling brave, the climb up the towers' 400 steps affords an interesting view over the rest of the cathedral. Finally, the museum in the crypt contains models, Gaudí's plans and numerous documents allowing you to follow the different stages of construction.

INFORMATION

Sagrada Família
(see p. 31)
C. Sicilia, 286
Metro Sagrada Família
☎ 93 207 30 31
Every day Sep.-Mar. 9am-6pm; 9am-7.15pm in summer.
Entrance charge.

The Cathedral

Dedicated to Saint Eulalie, one of the town's two patrons saints, Barcelona's Gothic cathedral was erected on the site of an ancient Paleo-Christian basilica, built in the 4th century – of which only the baptistery remains – and of an 11th-century Romanesque chapel. The construction of the cathedral began in 1298, but its façade was only completed in 1899, to the plans drawn in 1408 by French architect Charles Galtès.

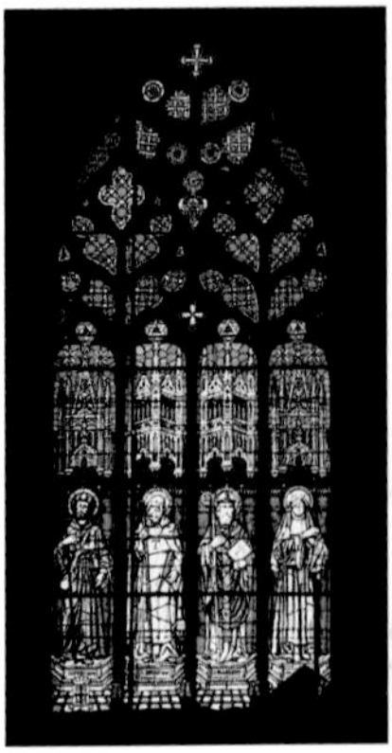

The interior

On both sides of the 24m- (80ft-) high nave, 28 chapels containing remarkable medieval Catalan paintings are sculpted with low-relief representations of *St Eulalie d'Ordónz' martyr*. Fifteenth-century stalls, reserved for the canons and bearing the coat of arms of the Order of the Golden Fleece, draw a half circle around the cathedral choir. The Capella de Sant Benet and Bernat Martorell's 15th-century retable are particularly remarkable. St Eulalie alabaster sarcophagus lies in the cathedral's crypt.

The cloister

Built between 1350 and 1448, the small rectangular-shaped cloister is a haven of peace, on the right side of the cathedral. Richly decorated chapels occupy three of its sides. Of interest are the wrought-iron fences from the 14th and 15th centuries, *The Lepante Christ* (16th century) in the Capella del Santíssim Sagrament and the statue of St. George, which decorates the fountain.

Religious feasts and traditions

On the day of St. Lucie (December 13), the cathedral square hosts a fair dedicated to Christmas decorations, and more specifically to small figurines representing the characters of the Nativity. Another tradition, just as popular, brings circles of dancers every Sunday at noon on the cathedral square to perform the *sardana*, a traditional Catalan dance.

INFORMATION

The Cathedral (see pp. 38-39)
Metro Jaume I
☎ 93 310 25 80
Free entrance every day 8am-1.15pm and 4.30-7pm
Entrance charge for the terrace and the museum every day 1.30-4.30pm.

Santa Maria del Mar

The Santa Maria del Mar church is located on a charming little square in the Ribera district, in the middle of a maze of streets which from the 13th to the 17th centuries provided the setting for jousts, tournaments, processions and various other celebrations. This old church, a meeting place for Gothic Barcelona's ship-owners and merchants, is one of the city's most sober and elegant monuments. Its construction, started in 1328 by the district's inhabitants, with the help of sailors, was completed within half a century. This speedy execution explains the building's exceptionally coherent style.

The interior

Santa Maria del Mar's three naves, which are of approximatively equal height, are separated by massive stone pillars. Its sumptuous stained-glass windows – among which the western rose window, representing the *Crowning of the Virgin*, is particularly beautiful – illuminate the lateral chapels. Having visited the church, you will not be surprised to learn that many consider it to be the finest achievement of Mediterranean Gothic architecture.

Exceptional acoustics

The extraordinary size of Santa Maria del Mar makes it an ideal concert hall. It is claimed that the echo generated within its huge structure will give the simplest melody a rich polyphonic texture.

The drama of 1428

As Northern Catalonia was shaken by numerous earthquakes between 1421 and 1433, the rose window of Santa Maria del Mar collapsed in 1428, killing several people.

INFORMATION

Santa Maria del Mar
(see p. 43)
Pl. Santa Maria
Metro Jaume I
Open every day 9am-1.30pm, 4.30-8pm, from 10am on Sun.
Entrance free.

The Palace of Music

In 1908, the Palace of Catalan Music was erected on the site of an abandoned monastery. Conceived by Lluís Domènech i Montaner, it has become the symbol of Catalan Modernisme, and represents the finest achievement of that period's decorative arts. In 1983, Òscar Tusquets restored and enlarged the building. In 1997, the palace became part of UNESCO's cultural Heritage of Humanity.

An audacious construction

Space being scarce, Domènech i Montaner demonstrated his resourcefulness in making best possible use of it. He set the rehearsal room at ground level and the concert hall on the first floor. He also imagined a half concealed laminated steel structure whose sturdy pillars could bear the weight of the arches.

The façade

Decorating the red brick façade, a group of sculptures by Miquel Blay is dedicated to Catalan popular music. A large ceramic freeze represents the singers of Lluis Bru's Orefeo while polychromic columns decorated with mosaics support the bust sculptures of great composers (Palestrina, Bach and Beethoven).

The concert hall

The light shining through the huge stained-glass windows of the inverted cupola, decorated with floral motifs, create an unforgettable atmosphere. In fact, this is the only concert hall in Europe to be illuminated by daylight. On each side of the stage are sculptures designed by Domènech i Montaner and executed by Pau Gargallo: a bust of Joseph Anselm Clavè (1824-1874) and one of Richard Wagner (1813-1883). The huge organ is surrounded by two balconies decorated with 18 statues of graceful feminine figures, each playing a musical instrument.

INFORMATION

Palace of Music
(see pp. 42-43)
Sant Francesc de Paula, 2
Metro Urquinaona
☎ 93 295 72 00
Open every day 10am-3.30pm, guided tour (charge) in English or Spanish (50 minutes) departure every 30 minutes.

The Güell Park

Far from the the town center's busy thoroughfares, a walk around Güell Park is like an enchanted journey through the world of the talented Gaudí. Located on a hill to the north of Barcelona, it offers a beautiful panoramic view over the city, the sea and the Sagrada Família, the artist's other monumental achievement.

A colossal project
In 1900, the industrialist Eusebi Güell had the idea to construct a residential complex composed of 60 private homes, a chapel, a factory and various areas dedicated to the leisurely pursuits of the community he intended to settle in this garden city. Antoni Gaudí took this opportunity to give free reign to his eccentricity. Unfortunately, due to financial difficulties, the project was abandoned prematurely. In 1923, the park became the property of the city and in 1984 was proclaimed a cultural Heritage of Humanity by the UNESCO.

A fantasy world
The main entrance to the park leads up a monumental staircase, covered in glass and ceramic mosaics, and into the hall of the hundred columns, whose ceilings are decorated with an extraordinary variety of objects, seemingly stuck together. Farther on, the Greek Theater, also known as the Theater of Nature, is surrounded by a huge swerving multicolored bench. As you take a stroll through the park, you will find at every turn fountains adorned with strange animals, grottoes, trees cut out of stone and extraordinary statues, such as that of a magnificent multicolored lizard.

The museum
Occupying the house which the artist inhabited between 1906 and 1926, during the early stages of the park's construction, the Casa Museu Gaudí is a wonderful collection of furniture, drawings and personal effects.

INFORMATION

Güell Park (see pp. 30-31)
Ctra. Carmel
☎ 93 315 11 11
Open every day 10am-6pm in winter; Mar. and Oct. 10am-7pm, 10am-8pm in summer.

Practicalities

Hotels

The city was lacking in luxury hotels before 1992, but since the Olympic Games a good range of accommodation catering to all tastes and budgets has appeared, with more than 150 hotels meeting the needs of its visitors. If you choose a hotel with sea views, you'll probably find it is in a quiet district, but a long way from the center. On the other hand, the city center is noisy and so it's best to ask for a room overlooking a courtyard. You may have a long walk to your hotel as many of th em are inaccessible by car.

Rates and conditions

The hotels listed in this guide are divided into four categories. The top three categories include telephone, TV and private bathrooms; the fourth is more basic. In general, breakfast isn't included in the price of rooms. A supplement is also charged for extra beds for children. There's no distinction between smoking and non-smoking rooms.
Rates for a double room before tax:

★★★★★	from €200
★★★★	between €120 and €200
★★★	between €90 and €120
★★	between €50 and €90

You will be charged an additional 7 percent tax (IVA) per night per room.
If you'd like the complete list of hotels in Barcelona, Contact the Gremi, Barcelona's central hotel booking office:
Via Laietana, 47 (08003),
☎ 93 301 62 40
Ⓕ 93 301 42 92.

You can make reservations in advance by phone or fax. You won't usually be asked for a deposit. Don't expect to have access to your room before noon, as it will not always be available. There is usually a charge for secure hotel parking.

Restaurants

Catalan cuisine tends to be fairly substantial and nourishing, but is not afraid of mixing flavors, so you'll find savory dishes containing nuts and fruit. As you may imagine from its proximity to the sea, fish and seafood figure heavily in restaurant menus, but meat is also good here. There are essentially three types of eating establishment: the *restaurante* (*restaurant* in Catalan), the *cafeteríà*, which tends to be cheaper than the restaurants, plus of course you can also order snacks in bars. Most restaurants will have a *menú del dia*, or daily set menu.

Tapas are small dishes of food, which used to be served free with drinks, but for which you now have to pay. *Raciones* are really just bigger portions of *tapas*.

A *bodega* (literally "cellar"), *cerveceria* (*cervesseria* in Catalan), *tasca* (*tasques*) and *taberna* are all types of bar (see p. 13).

In summer, you'll be well advised to make for the port or high parts of the city (Tibidabo) to benefit from any slight breeze, though there are also many shaded terraces in the city center. Generally speaking, you don't need to make reservations in advance, unless you decide to visit one of the trendiest restaurants, in which case, you can ask your hotel receptionist to call for you. There's no formal dress code and you can wear whatever you like – a tie isn't compulsory anywhere.

However, the people of Barcelona always make every effort to look their best.

"Weekend" rates to look out for

Many hotels also operate a "*fin de semana*" price, or "weekend" rate, which is extremely advantageous, since it allows you a discount of up to 50 percent of the normal price. It's in your interest to select a higher-category hotel that grants this discount, as you'll pay the same price as you would for an average hotel without discount. Always ask at the time of booking or you can also get information from:

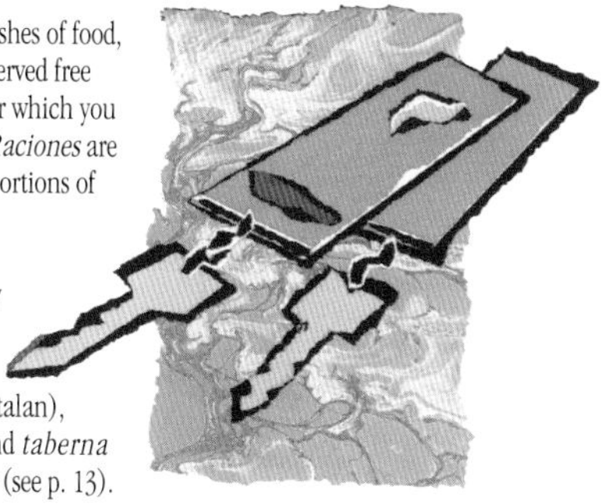

Tourist Information Office
Plaça de Catalunya, 17-S (basement)
☎ 93 368 97 30
Open every day 9am-9pm.

Tourist bureau
Plaça Sant Jaume
Open Mon.-Sat. 10am-8pm, Sun. 10am-2pm.
This office will help you reserve a hotel at the "*fin de semana*" rates (operating in 35 selected hotels) and will provide you with a BIP (Barcelona Important Person) card, which gives you discounts at restaurants, museums, shows, car rental firms, etc. The advantageous "*fin de semana*" prices operate throughout the year at the weekend (Fri.-Sun.), and every day from June 21 to September 11, and are definitely worth looking out for. There's no need to send payment in advance – you pay the hotel direct.

WHEN DO WE EAT?

Spain has its own special mealtimes, with lunch served from 1.30 to 3pm and dinner from 9 or 10 to 11.30pm. Don't arrive too early or you'll come across the staff having their meals. Nearly all restaurants accept credit cards. Although a tip isn't mandatory and is not usually included on the bill in Spain, it is thoughtful to leave 10 percent of the bill, but anything more is considered excessive.

Hotels

1 - Claris
2 - Romàntic (p. 89)
3 - Condes de Barcelona

Port Olímpic

Arts Barcelona★★★★★

Carrer Marina, 19-21
☎ 93 221 10 00
Ⓕ 93 221 10 71
Metro Ciutadella Vila Olímpica.

A hotel beside the sea where businessmen and others find elegant hi-tech rooms and suites with an uninterrupted view of the bay and Port Olímpic. *Bar Terraza* and a swimming pool to top up your suntan.

Eixample

Claris★★★★★

Carrer Pau Claris, 150
☎ 93 487 62 62
Ⓕ 93 215 79 70
www.derbyhotels.es
Metro Passeig de Gràcia.

The former palace of the Counts of Vedruna appeals particularly to travelers who appreciate its collection of ancient Egyptian artifacts. Each of its 120 rooms is decorated with antiques, paintings and 17th-century English or *Modernista* furniture. There is a private bar.

Ritz★★★★★

Gran Via de les Corts Catalanes, 668
☎ 93 318 52 00
Ⓕ 93 318 01 48
Metro Urquinaona.

A delightful place to spend an evening, where Salvador Dalí once demanded a suite for the statue of his horse. A special weekend offer (subject to availability) at this charming, traditional hotel is temptation enough.

Alexandra★★★★

Carrer Mallorca, 251
☎ 93 467 71 66
Ⓕ 93 488 02 58
Metro Diagonal.

A convenient place to stay close to the city's shops, with 75 wood-decorated designer rooms. A room overlooking the courtyard will give you an idea of the magnificence of the houses in l'Eixample.

Condes de Barcelona★★★★

Passeig de Gràcia, 73-75
☎ 93 488 22 00
F 93 467 47 81
Metro Diagonal.

This *Modernista* building has been brilliantly renovated, preserving the classical Romano-Moorish stairwell, and you'll receive a courteous welcome. Ask for a room overlooking the garden at the back of the hotel if you're looking for peace and quiet during your stay.

Duques de Bergara★★★★

Carrer Bergara, 11
☎ 93 301 51 51
F 93 317 34 42
Metro Catalunya.

You'll love this turn-of-the-last-century former private mansion, just a stone's throw from Plaça de Catalunya, especially the sumptuous marble entrance and staircase. The convenient parking lot is a bonus.

Gran Hotel Havana★★★★

Gran Via de les Corts Catalanes, 647
☎ 93 412 11 15
F 93 412 26 11
Metro Girona.

The hotel's turn-of-the-last-century façade is reminiscent of the grand hotels of the seaside resorts of San Sebastian. The 145 luxurious rooms are provided with every comfort – satellite TV, air-conditioning, safe, etc. Centrally located and ideal if you like shopping.

St Moritz★★★★

Carrer Diputación, 262
☎ 93 412 15 00
F 93 412 12 36
Metro Passeig de Gràcia.

A very central hotel with an interior garden that's a bonus in summer. The neoclassical façade is impressive, as is the size of the rooms equipped with satellite TV. The service is attentive and there's a fitness center if you have enough energy after shopping in the neighboring *passeig*.

Barrio Gótico

Colon★★★★

Avinguda Catedral, 7
☎ 93 301 14 04
F 93 317 29 15
Metro Jaume I or Catalunya.

A hotel frequented by Miró opposite the cathedral. Ask for a room with a balcony overlooking the square so you can follow the movements of the Sunday *sardanas* (Catalan dancing). Its location is ideal for exploring the Barrio Gótico.

Regencia Colon★★★

Carrer Sagristans, 13-17
☎ 93 318 98 58
F 93 317 28 22
Metro Jaume I.

This hotel, a stone's throw from the cathedral, is less luxurious than the Colon (see left) but has the advantage of being in a quiet pedestrian area. It's a good place to come as a family – children can play in the cathedral square.

Metropol★★★

Carrer Ample, 31
☎ 93 310 51 00
F 93 319 12 76
Metro Drassanes.

Near Port Vell and at the lower end of the Barrio Gótico, this hotel offers unbeatable value for money. The foyer has retained the character of a private town house, and the rooms are small but secluded. An opportunity you certainly won't want to miss if you're on a budget.

Nouvel★★★

Carrer Santa Anna, 20
☎ 93 301 82 74
F 93 301 83 70
Metro Catalunya.

The *Modernista* setting of this hotel, a small street in the Barrio Gótico, isn't lacking in charm. Its carved ceilings, old *azulejos* and elegant stairwell make it a delightful place to stay, especially for visitors who have a particular interest in authentic Art Deco.

Jardi★★★

Plaça Sant Josep Oriol, 1
☎ 93 301 59 00
F 93 318 36 64
Metro Liceu.

The Jardi is wonderfully located in the beating heart of the city, the Plaça del Pi pedestrian area. The rooms overlook pine trees and street entertainers of all kinds. It's a small but reasonably priced hotel and very popular in this category.

Diagonal

Rey Juan Carlos I★★★★★

Avinguda Diagonal, 661
☎ 93 364 40 40
🅕 93 364 42 64
Metro Zona Universitaria.

This was the last hotel to open in 1992 and heads of state from around the world stayed here during the Olympic Games. Its cavernous foyer is impressive, and the 412 rooms are arranged round it as if it were an ocean liner. A little remote from the city center , however the hotel makes up for this by having room for gardens, terraces and a pool.

Gran Derby★★★★

Carrer Loreto, 28
☎ 93 322 20 62
🅕 93 419 68 20
Metro Hospital Clinic.

To judge from the brick façade, you'd think you were in Chelsea in London, yet the delightful sun-lit garden leaves you in little doubt – you are indeed in Barcelona, near the Turò Park district, with its luxurious shop windows. The hotel has ultramodern split-level rooms and staff will go out of their way to rent cars, and reserve tickets for concerts and excursions to Montserrat for you.

Ramblas

Rivoli Ramblas★★★★

Las Ramblas, 128
☎ 93 302 66 43
🅕 93 318 87 60
Metro Catalunya.

At the top of the Ramblas, this 1930s building, restored in an original way, has given each of its 90 rooms a distinctive touch – antiques dealers, young designers and artists were involved in the project. The hotel is in a very good location, but there is no parking lot.

Méridien Barcelona★★★

Las Ramblas, 111
☎ 93 318 62 00
🅕 93 301 77 76
Metro Catalunya.

This hotel, in the heart of the Ramblas, is a favorite with celebrities, including Bruce Springsteen, The Rolling Stones, Oasis and Placido Domingo. It has 206 comfortable and sophisticated rooms offering all the facilities a star could want.

Hotel Montecarlo★★★

Las Ramblas, 124
☎ 93 412 04 04
🅕 93 318 73 23
Metro Catalunya.

In the heart of the Ramblas district, the ideal starting point for walks through the Barrio Gótico and the Raval areas. Behind its early 20th-century façade, are 55 rooms, with contemporary design, some with a Jacuzzi. Staff at the reception desk are very kind and helpful.

Raval

Sant Agusti★★★

Plaça Sant Agusti, 3
☎ 93 318 16 58
🅕 93 317 29 28
Metro Liceu.

In a shady, peaceful square close to the Ramblas, the Sant Agusti hotel is located beside St. Augustine's church. Ask for the attic rooms, with exposed beams,

1 - Romàntic
2 - Rivoli Ramblas
3 - Hotel Montercarlo

which are quite delightful. There's a handy parking lot in the area too.

España★★

Carrer Sant Pau, 9-11
☎ 93 318 17 58
Ⓕ 93 317 11 34
Metro Liceu.

To fans of Art Nouveau, the dining rooms by Domenech i Montaner are quite irresistible. Set in the heart of the Barrio Chino, the España keeps alive memories of a bygone age – but the decor in the dining room is more memorable than the food. The bedrooms are spacious and comfortable. Ask for a room overlooking the indoor patio.

Sitges

San Sebastian★★★★

Port Alegre, 53
☎ 93 894 86 76
Ⓕ 93 894 04 30.

Opposite the small bay of San Sebastian, the hotel's 51 spruce rooms are both pleasant and practical. With the sunny terrace inviting you to relax and enjoy your stay, it's just the place to satisfy your longing for idleness and the beach (see pp. 70-71).

El Xalet★★

C. Isla de Cuba, 35
☎ 93 811 00 70
Ⓕ 93 894 55 79.

This beautifully preserved *Modernista* villa is set in a luxuriant garden with a pool. The ten rooms contain a rather motley collection of furniture. The friendly welcome and food lovingly prepared by the owner rom fresh market produce, are sure to please those seeking a quiet setting (see p. 71).

Romàntic★★

Carrer Sant Isidre, 33
☎ 93 894 83 75
Ⓕ 93 894 81 67
Closed in winter.

Three *Modernista* houses were saved to create this hotel (interior pictured above left). Visitors can enjoy the patio, planted with palm trees, and share the owner's nostalgia for Modernisme. Ask for a peaceful room with a balcony overlooking the garden for the lovely view.

Restaurants

1

2

3

1 - *La Verónica (p. 93)*
2 - *Sempronia*
3 - *Agua (p. 92)*

Barrio Gótico

Hostal El Pintor★★

Carrer St. Honorat, 7
☎ 93 301 40 65
Metro Jaume I
Open every day.

This hotel is pleasantly located behind the cathedral, with the emphasis on trendy and decor – exposed bricks and beams and gleaming floor tiles. They serve traditional Catalan cuisine – asparagus with marinated salmon, and hake with leeks grilled the old-fashioned way.

El Gran Café★

Carrer d'Avinyò, 9
☎ 93 318 79 86
Metro Liceu
Closed Sun. and public hols.

El Gran Café's copper coffee percolator, black-and-white checked floor tiles, *bistrot* tables and starched tablecloths, put you in mind of fin-de-siècle Paris. Senor Ramon will be only to pleased to show you his connoisseur's wine cellar (*bodega*), if you ask him. The set lunch is €7.20.

Pou Dols★★

Baixada de Sant Miquel, 6
☎ 93 412 05 79
Open Mon.-Sat.

Pou Dols' menu is varied and delicious – consommé with liver mousse, sardine tart with young garlic, white fish with parmesan, and boned pig's trotters with artichokes. With an inventive menu and a sober decor by Starck and Maurer, this is a very popular place. After sampling some of these gourmet dishes you will doubtless be added to its list of fans. Not far from the Ajuntament (Town Hall). Allow around €24 per person.

Eixample

Casa Calvet★★★

Carrer de Casp, 48
☎ 93 412 40 12
Metro Urquinaona
Closed Sun. & public hols.

Set in one of the houses built by Gaudí (see p. 30), which used to house a textile business, Casa

;alvet resembles a loft with vooden beams and traditionally tuccoed walls. Among the chef's ecommendations are tasty ockle salad, delicious fresh asagne with scampi, melting illet of sole with cava, and nouth-watering white chocolate nousse.

Semproniana★★

Carrer de Rosselló, 148
☎ 93 453 18 20
Metro Diagonal.

'his former printing factory ffers a charming setting for iners in a cosy candlelit tmosphere among antique furiture. The creative Catalancuiine includes black sausageasagne and "Delirium remens" – a wonderfully wicked hocolate dessert.

Madrid-Barcelona★★★

Carrer d'Aragò, 282
☎ 93 215 70 26
Metro Passeig de Gràcia
Closed Sun. and public hols.

Iot very far from the Tàpies oundation, this former rain station has been onverted into a *tapas* bar servng omelettes, squid and egglants (aubergines) – with a lice of nostalgia thrown in.

Flash-Flash★

Granada del Penedès, 25
☎ 93 237 09 90
Metro Diagonal
Open every day 1pm-1am.

A popular meeting spot for trendy Barcelona society, Flash-Flash is a rather glamorous venue, decorated with black-and-white photos and pop art. Enjoy a selection of omelettes or the best hamburgers in town. The service is faultless, and the post-midnight "Menu Golfo" is good value at €9.50.

Port and Barceloneta

Els Pescadors★★★

Plaça Prim, 1
☎ 93 225 20 18
Metro Poble Nou
Open every day.

This terrace beyond the Olympic Village is a delightful place to enjoy the mild air. Opt for the marble-tabled "antigua" room rather than the more impersonal "moderna," and try oven-grilled peppers, black rice with ink, and cod with honey.

Barceloneta★★

L'Escar, 22 Moll dels Pescadors
☎ 93 221 21 11
Metro Barceloneta
Open every day.

For armchair sailors. Wood, rope and coarse sailcloth create a nautical atmosphere in this fashionable restaurant overlooking Port Vell. Picture windows, duckboards, wood paneling and red-and-blue striped canvas tablecloths help to whet the appetite as surely as the sea air.

Cal Pinxo★★

Carrer de Baluard, 124
Platja Barceloneta
☎ 93 221 50 28
Metro Barceloneta
Closed Sun. evening and Mon.

With *chiringuitos* (see p. 63) a thing of the past, the Cal Pinxo restaurant carries on the tradition of the kiosks and fishermen's restaurants, serving *fideus a la cassola*, *paella* with pasta, *mariscos*, seafood and monkfish in *cazuela* with ailloli sauce.

Carballeira★★

Carrer de Reina Cristina, 3
☎ 93 310 10 06
Metro Barceloneta
Closed Sun. evening, Mon. and public hols.

An excellent fish restaurant that makes no concessions to fashion. Plenty of local color, with portholes, model ships and turtles – an endearing popular classic according to some, an affront according to others. Judge for yourself.

Reial Club Marítim★★

Moll d'Espanya
☎ 93 221 62 56
Metro Barceloneta
Closed Sun. evening.

Turning its back on the hi-tech Maremagnum, this little place is like an officers' club from another era. The view of the overhead bridge, Rambla de Mar, and the steamers setting off for the islands only adds to the atmosphere, and the culinary delights – bass in rosemary, fish soup and pasta with prawns – are wonderful.

Agua★★

Passeig Marítim de la Barceloneta, 30
☎ 93 206 06 58
Metro Barceloneta.
Open lunchtime: Mon.-Fri. 1.30-4pm (to 5pm Sat. & Sun.); evenings: Mon.-Sun. 8.30pm-midnight (to 1am Fri. & Sat.).

This is an idyllic spot, with its sea-and-sky-blue decor, for an apéritif or fresh seafood, simply prepared. There's a pleasant atmosphere, a delightful sea view at lunchtime and a romantic ambience at night under the stars.

The city heights

A Contraluz★★

Carrer del Milanesat, 19, near Via Augusta, Doctor Roux
☎ 93 203 06 58
Take a taxi
Open every day.

The setting and summer terrace of this Tragaluz restaurant (see pp. 54-55) will make you forget the city. Try the delicious risotto with boletus mushrooms, foie gras with baby onions, or potato and vine-leaf puffs. As in most restaurants, you can try this tasty Catalan cuisine more cheaply from the lunch menu (€13.80).

La Balsa★★

Carrer de la Infanta Isabel, 4
☎ 93 211 50 48
Av. Tibidabo train station
Closed Sun. and Mon.

A restaurant nestling on the Tibidabo hillside, with a straw awning that complements the greenery. Designed by Tusquets, it won a prize in 1979. With comfortable sofas and a choice of books, it's a delightfully relaxing place. Try the hake tartare and red-fruit sorbet which are as light as air.

Can Travi Nou★★

Cami Antic de Sant Cebrià
☎ 93 428 03 01
Take a taxi
Closed Sun. evening.

This Catalan property in the city heights has the look of a family home. A climbing vine twines round the pergola, where the guests sit and savor the delights of country cooking. If you warm to Latin charm, give your order to the Brylcreemed waiter.

La Venta★★

Plaça del Doctor Andreu
☎ 93 212 64 55
Take a taxi
Closed Sun.

This pastel-colored open-air café perched on top of the Tibidabo still has a late 19th-century air and old-fashioned charm. It's the ideal place for couples, who can huddle up to the stove in winter or dream on the terrace in summer while sharing a *matò de panses amb melles*, a sweet made from honey and currants.

El Asador de Aranda★★

Avinguda del Tibidabo, 31
☎ 93 417 01 15
Take a taxi
Closed Sun. evening.

You come here for the decor – the Moorish entrance to this *Modernista* house is like a harem. In summer, on the terrace, they invariably serve shoulder of lamb grilled in an old-fashioned charcoal oven. Before leaving, climb the tower for the fabulous view.

Atlantic Restaurant★★

Av. Luis Montades, 8
☎ 93 418 52 04
Open Mon.-Sat.

The Atlantic has a marvelou[s] view over the Mediterranean. Ad[d] to this a menu full of sophisticated flavors and you won't regret having come this far. Ther[e] are mussels stuffed with liver, ric[e] with clams, sole stuffed wit[h] prawns in oyster sauce, and duc[k] with raspberries (€30-42).

Bonanova★

Carrer de Sant Gervasi de Cassoles, 103
☎ 93 417 10 33
Plaça J. Folguera train station
Closed Sun. evening and Mon.

This family restaurant is reminiscent of a 1900s gaming roo[m]. The *Modernista* decor of colored *azulejos*, black-and-whit[e] tiled floor and tarnished mirror[s] hasn't aged a bit. From rabb[it] and snails to tasty fried fish, th[e] menu wavers between land an[d] sea. Worth the detour.

Ribera

El Salero★

Carrer del Rec, 60
☎ 93 319 80 22
Metro Jaume 1
Closed Sat. & Sun.

The trendy and chic frequen[t] this café/bar/restaurant, wit[h] its "New York"-style-interio[r] and relaxed atmosphere. Th[e] white decor is dotted wit[h] objects found in London fle[a] markets, and there's a ver[y] cosmopolitan atmospher[e]. Enjoy tasty tartares, dessert[s], salads and excellent musi[c].

Arrel★★

Carrer Fusina, 5
☎ 93 319 92 99
Metro Jaume 1
Open Mon.-Sat. 8.30am-11pm.

This loft, with its rather severe decor of white bricks and

1 - Reial Club Maritím (p. 91)
2 - La Balsa
3 - Cal Pep

luminum bar, is the latest lace to see and be seen. There s a good bar menu, and if ou're planning a round of the ars in Plaça Del Born it's the leal place to start.

Cal Pep★★

laça de les Olles, 8
☎ 93 319 61 83
Metro Jaume I
Closed Sun. and Mon. unch.

t Ribera you have to stand at he *barra* (bar) to try out the hef's various suggestions. He oncocts fried food and dishes of he day – *supions* and *tellines*, *ulpitos* and shellfish – right efore your eyes.

Raval

Casa Leopoldo★★★

Carrer Sant Rafael, 24
☎ 93 441 30 14
Metro Liceu
Closed Sun. evening and Mon.

n rooms decorated with ellow and blue azulejos tiles), you'll be served the best *à amb tomaquet* (see p. 10) in the city, as well as fried young fish, prawns and scampi. The customary presence of famous writers Vázquez Montalbán, Marsé and Mendoza may explain the relation between cost and quality. Perhaps it's the price of fame.

Ramblas

La Véronica★

Carrer d'Avinyò, 30
☎ 93 412 11 22
Metro Liceu
Open Wed.-Sun. noon-1am, Tue. 8pm-1.30am.

Noisy and fashionable, this restaurant and pizzeria is a great people-watching spot. The food is surprisingly good and includes Gorgonzola and apple-flavored pizzas, tasty quiches and delicious desserts.

Quinze Nits★

Plaça Reial, 6
☎ 93 317 30 75
Metro Drassanes
Open every day.

Living on its past reputation of good quality and price, under the arches of the Plaça Reial, this popular venue is not as good as it once was. The €5.98 menu is one of the better deals, however, but be prepared to wait.

Sitges

Maricel★★

Passeig de la Ribera, 6
☎ 93 894 20 54.
Closed Tue. evening and Wed.

On the *paseo* (promenade) facing the bay, the terrace between sea and sky (*mar i cel*) Maricel serves classic Mediterranean cuisine – *paella marinera*, *escalivada*, sweet peppers, eggplants (aubergines), and onions marinated in olive oil.

Cafés and tea rooms

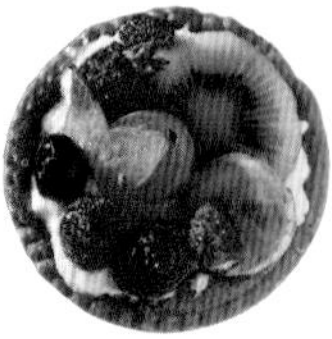

2

1 - La Estrella Sitges
2 - Mauri
3 - El Taxidermista

3

Ciutadella

Hivernacle Café

Parc de la Ciutadella
Passeig Picasso
☎ 93 295 40 17
Metro Ciutadella
Open Mon.-Sat. 10am-midnight, Sun. 10am-5pm.

A greenhouse dating from the Great Exhibition of 1888 has become the most romantic summer garden café, with luxuriant plants, purring cats and even a melodious fountain which echoes the live jazz played there on Wednesdays.

Ramblas

Bar Jardin

Carrer de la Portaferissa, 17
Metro Liceu.

Take me to the Casbah! A camel and oasis create an exotic atmosphere. There are also little garden tables and pop-art sofas which all add up to an interesting mix of styles and a haven for the young.

Raval

Granja Viader

Carrer d'En Xuclà, 4
☎ 93 318 34 86
Metro Catalunya
Closed Sun. and Mon. morning.

Granja has found the formul for a tea room to please all age from children to little old ladie and from creative types to peo ple laden with shopping bag Here's where you'll find the be crème brûlée, Swiss chocolat with whipped cream and home made lemon madeleines i the city.

Horchateria Sirvent

Carrer de Parlament, 56
☎ 93 441 27 20
Metro Sant Antoni
Open every day.

Slake your thirst near the Rond San Pau with *horchata*, barle water, or a *turròn*-flavored ic cream (see p. 125). People trad itionally hesitate betwee *ranizada*, coffee-flavored, rushed ice, and a delicious ice-ream cornet. You can worry bout your diet tomorrow!

Barrio Gótico

3on Mercat

3aixada de la Llibreteria, -3
☎ 93 315 29 08
Metro Jaume I
Closed Sun.

or €0.57 you can savor a strong lack coffee, or *tallat* with a dash f milk, with the heady aroma of Guatemalan coffee, Ethiopian nocca or *gran altura mezcla*. Drink your choice standing at the rowded bar with a tasty *ocadillo*.

El Taxidermista

Plaça Reial, 8
☎ 93 317 06 97
Metro Liceu
Open Tue.-Sun. 10am-.30am.

he former natural history mu-eum has been extensively and uccessfully renovated and now ouses a remarkable café and estaurant with a cosmopolitan tmosphere and a sophisticated, ntellectual clientèle. The nterior is a subtle mix of *Modernista* and contemporary esign, and it's a good spot for reakfast, a selection of *tapas* or n appetizing Mediterranean neal. You'll receive a friendly velcome and enjoy a great view f Plaça Reial. Lunch menus ange from €6-7.20.

3ar del Pi

Plaça Sant Josep Oriol, 1
☎ 93 302 21 23
Metro Liceu
Open every day.

he Bar del Pi is the most pleas-nt and charming café in the ity. Intellectuals, the "divine eft," and artists short of inspiration come here. Newspapers are available for customers to read and the noise of the coffee percolator makes a change from the sounds of jazz in the square.

El Café d'Estiu

Plaça Sant Lu, 5
☎ 93 310 30 14
Metro Jaume I
Open Tue.-Sun. 7-10pm.

In summer, a few tables are set up near a refreshing pool in the courtyard of the F. Marès Museum, in the heart of the Barrio Gótico. Large white parasols and a wooden stall offer visitors a delicious break in a quiet haven.

Laie

Carrer de Pau Claris, 85
☎ 93 318 17 39
Metro Urquinaona
Open Mon.-Fri. 10am-9pm, Sat. 10.30am-9pm.

For a literary and gourmet break, this tea room-cum-bookshop is a dream come true. Magazines from all over the world, art books and philosophical treatises mingle with homemade pastries and the smell of coffee. It's a perfect blend of nourishment for body and soul.

Mauri

Rambla de Catalunya, 103
☎ 93 215 09 98
Metro Diagonal
Open every day (closed Sun. 3-5pm).

Smart young mothers with babies and well-dressed ladies come here to indulge their sweet tooth. A confectioners and cake shop where perfect taste, elaborate display shelves and black and gold window displays are the order of the day.

La Estrella Sitges

Carrer Major, 52
☎ 93 894 00 79
Closed Mon.

This patisserie is decorated from floor to ceiling with frescoes, bottles of liqueur and boxes of sweets. Traditional treats await you in the *salò de té* – why not try a little glass of Sitges malmsey, the local liqueur, as well?

Ribera

El Xampanyet

Carrer de Montcada, 22
☎ 93 319 70 03
Metro Jaume I
Open Tue.-Sat. noon-4pm, 6.30-11.30pm, Sun. 6.30-11.30pm.

A small, friendly inn run by the same family since 1929. Colorful *azulejos*, flasks and wine barrels set the tone. The anchovies, olives and marinated fish served with Penedès white wine are delicious, but watch the bill.

Practicalities

The people of Barcelona have a nose for business – hardly surprising since the city was founded on commerce, and trading has taken place here for 2,000 years. So no need to worry, there are shops on every street corner.

You'll find the most stylish shops (selling jewelry, designer labels and luxury clothes) on the Passeig de Gràcia, Rambla de Catalunya and in the area around the Turò park. Arts and crafts and small businesses liven up the old quarters (Barrio Gótico and Ribera), the Boqueria market on the Ramblas opens very early in the morning and the port attracts many shoppers as well with the new Maremagnum center, which is also open on Sundays.

Shop opening hours

Most shops open Monday to Saturday, 10am to 2pm and 4.30 to 8pm, with food shops opening an hour earlier in the morning. Make a note of the opening hours if you don't want to get caught out – all the shops close for lunch, with the exception of the big shopping centers, Illà on the Diagonal and Corte Inglès in the Plaça de Catalunya, which stay open all day long.
Some shops close on Saturday afternoons, but the Maremagnum shopping center located in the port is open from 11am to 11pm.

SALES

The majority of shops hold their sales from the second week in January to the end of February and in July and August. They're not as spectacular as the London sales, but you can usually find reductions of anything from 25 to 50 percent, except at Zara (clothes), where the prices are really slashed.

Paying for your purchases

Most shopkeepers accept credit cards (American Express, MasterCard and Visa International) and, of course, cash. You just present your card and sign the till receipt in the usual way. In the event of loss or theft, call the relevant center in Madrid:

American Express
☎ 900 810 029
F 91 570 19 97

Diners
☎ 91 701 59 00
F 91 523 32 03

Eurocard, MasterCard and Visa
☎ 91 519 21 00
F 91 346 55 12.
Traveler's checks are commonly accepted.

Prices are displayed everywhere and it isn't the done thing to bargain, apart from in flea markets, where you'll find that the Catalans are tough negotiators and every penny counts. So, be firm, forewarned is forearmed!

You can apply for a visitor's shopping card (see p. 35) from:

Turisme de Barcelona
Plaça de Catalunya, 17 (basement)
☎ 93 368 97 30
www.barcelonaturisme.com

This card provides certain benefits (including discounts of around 10 percent) in more than 200 shops where the sign "*Barcelona, ciutat de compres*" ("Barcelona, the shoppers' paradise") is displayed in the window. It's definitely worth getting if you're planning to do a lot of shopping.

Customs duty on purchases

If you're a citizen of a member state of the European Union, you won't have to pay any customs duty on your purchases, whatever their value, but you will have to show the receipts. Non EU-citizens are exempt from paying sales tax (IVA) on purchases with a value of more than €90.15. Remember to ask for a "Tax-free check" when making your purchase.
On leaving Spain, make sure you have the checks stamped at customs so that you can cash them at a branch of the Banco Exterior de España when you arrive home.
If you buy a work of art or antique declared as *de valor patrimonial* ("of national value"), you must request an export license from the Spanish equivalent of the National Heritage. The vendor will help you with this process. You can insist on a certificate of authenticity. An invoice is always essential – you can be asked for it at customs and it will be useful to you if you want to sell your purchase at a later date, or if you're burgled and need to fill in a claim form for your insurance company.
Be on the lookout for forgeries and stolen goods. If you export one of the latter, you could be prosecuted for possession of stolen goods. Buy only from established traders and be wary of anything that looks too much of a bargain. Customs: Passeig Josep Carner 27, (☎ 93 443 30 08).

TRANSPORT FACILITIES

If you buy a piece of furniture or bulky object, there's no problem about having it delivered home. Simply give the delivery company a photocopy of your invoice, and they'll make out the delivery note.
UPS, United Parcel Service
freephone ☎ 900 10 24 10
www.ups.com
This haulier makes deliveries worldwide and can arrange immediate dispatch if required.
RUNNER ☎ 93 309 79 50. They accept packages in all sizes and will supply a free quotation for deliveries in Spain.
GEFCO ☎ 93 729 79 70.
This large company offers both a national and an international parcel service. They will also take urgent deliveries.

Women's fashion:
ready-to-wear, accessories, shoes and designer clothes

You may dream of being a *Barefoot Contessa*, or stealing the show in *High Society*. You may aspire to taking *Breakfast at Tiffany's*, while in search of *La Dolce Vita*, but if if you find yourself attending *Four Weddings and a Funeral* you will certainly need some *Pret-à-Porter*. Cinematic fantasies apart, if you'd like to inject a little Spanish style into your wardrobe, here are some places you should try.

Forum

C. de Ferlandina, 31
☎ 93 441 80 18
Open Tue.-Sat.
10.30am-2pm,
5-8.30pm

Just a step away from the Museum of Contemporary Art, the work of 60 jewelry designers is on display in this workshop/gallery and shop which is run by a young German woman. The stunning pieces are made in limited editions and prices range from €24-600. If you're a lover of unique, contemporary jewelry, make sure you come here, and don't forget to take a look at the workshop to see how it's all made.

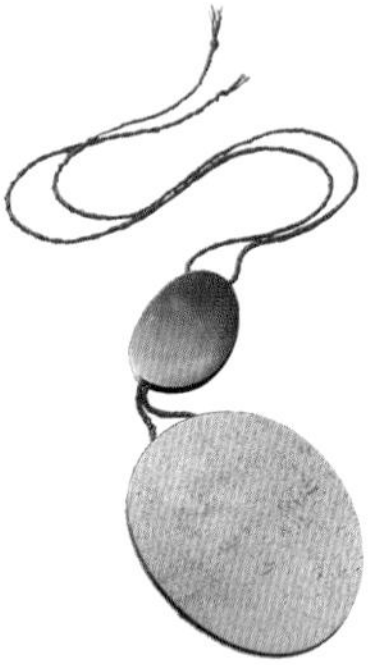

Muxart

C. de Rosselló, 230
☎ 93 488 10 64
Open Mon.-Sat.
10am-2pm, 4.30-8.30pm.

Muxart is an outstanding Catalan designer who excels in the art of making boots, both with and without laces. Made in Menorca, they're distinctive for the detail of the finish and the quality of the materials. If you're looking for originality you've come to the right place. Expect to pay €120-138.

Loewe

Passeig de Gràcia, 35
☎ 93 216 04 00
Metro Passeig de Gràcia
Open Mon.-Sat. 9.30am-8pm.

Loewe uses the elegant façade of the Casa Lléo Morera as a setting for its luxury leather goods. Like its first cousins Gucci and Hermès, Loewe supplies top-of-the-range goods. With its 150-year tradition of quality and luxury, the company has all the know-how needed to produce stylish, distinctive leather articles and colorful, elegant silk scarves.

Groc

C. de Muntaner, 385
☎ 93 202 30 77
Open Mon.-Sat. 10am-2pm, 4.30-8.30pm.

One of the first places to have sold clothes by designers such as Antonio Miró, for both men and women. Groc has introduced its own label and

offers a choice of sophisticated, elegant garments made of cotton, linen and silk in fluid simple shapes and designs.

Casa Oliveras

C. de la Dagueria, 11
☎ 93 315 19 05
Metro Jaume I
Open Mon.-Fri. 9am-1pm, 4-7pm.

Who says Catalan embroidery has gone out of style? Behind the cathedral, in a shop with unusual porcelain lamp-shades, Rosa embroiders decorative detail that will give ordinary dresses a somewhat antique look.

El Mercadillo

C. de la Portaferissa, 17
☎ 93 317 85 64
Metro Catalunya
Open Mon.-Sat. 10.30am-8pm.

With a cardboard camel and New Age music to greet you, you'll know you're in an unusual shop. The owner sells a combination of streetwear, casual clothes and secondhand items, including a cool look for psychedelic evenings – platform shoes, fluorescent skirts, ponchos and shirts made of African fabrics – to suit those who like to be a little different.

Casa Ciutad

Avinguda del Portal de l'Angel, 14
☎ 93 317 04 33
Open Mon.-Fri. 10.30am-9pm, Sat. 10am-9pm.

Since 1892, the company has supplied *articulos de tocador* (toiletry articles), including a formidable array of brushes and combs, some of them Spanish-style, to hold complicated hairdos in place (€21-84).

LA MANUAL ALPARGATERA

Carrer d'Avinyò, 7
☎ 93 301 01 72
Metro Liceu
Open Mon.-Sat. 9.30am-1.30pm, 4.30-8pm.

Behind a whitewashed façade lie handmade espadrilles and sandals of every shape and size – boot-style, with laces or embroidery, colored and striped. The workshop is on the premises and you can order a pair made-to-measure from the owner, who supplies the likes of actor Jack Nicholson. You can even buy mini-espadrilles for a new baby (€3-3.60).

Lydia Delgado

Carrer de Minerva, 21
☎ 93 415 99 98
Metro Diagonal
Open Mon.-Fri. 9am-2pm, 4.30-8.30pm, Sat. 10am-2pm, 4.30-8.30pm.

This young Spanish designer shows her chic, sexy clothes in a 1950s setting, with suits priced from €600, as well as 1960s Cubist dresses and hipster trousers – all are up-to-date styles as dynamic as their designer.

Julie Sohn

C. de Consell de Cent, 30
☎ 93 487 84 24
Open Mon.-Sat. 10.30am-8.30pm.

Julie Sohn, a young Korean designer, creates demure styles more reminiscent of Jil Sander than Jean-Paul Gaultier. Made in Barcelona, the raw wool suits and poplin shirts create a no-frills, trendy traditional look (a suit costs €360-430).

Atalanta

Passeig del Born, 10
☎ 93 268 37 02
Metro Jaume 1 or Barceloneta
Open Mon.-Sun. 10.30am-2,30pm, 4.30-8pm, closed Mon. afternoon

Judith Gaccimo and Claudio Mendee are the creators of these New-Age conceptual scarves. Huge, highly original and hand-painted, they are hard to resist, even if they are relatively expensive. In any case, the shop is well worth a visit, if only for the pleasure of the eyes.

Joieria Sunyer

Gran Via de les Corts Catalanes, 660
☎ 93 317 22 93
Metro Urquinaona
Open Mon.-Fri. 10am-1.30pm, 4.30-8pm.

Since 1835, five generations of jewelers have succeeded one another in this Art-Deco setting opposite the Ritz, a magnificent showcase for gilded silver bracelets (€360) and jewelry in exclusive designs passed down from father to son. A custom jewelers, it provides an old-fashioned service.

Notémon

Carrer de Pau Claris, 159
☎ Ⓕ 93 487 60 84
Metro Passeig de Gràcia
Open Tue.-Sat. 10.30am-2pm, 4.30-8.30pm, closed Mon. & Sun.

You'll find a selection of modern clothes for both men and women in this original shop, with its light and airy white interior. The collections range from classic to the latest styles, and even vintage. The choice is up to you.

Jean Pierre Bua

Avinguda Diagonal, 469
☎ 93 439 71 00
Metro Diagonal
Open Mon.-Sat. 10am-2pm, 4.30-8.30pm.

With sexy layering, sophisticated recycling and scandalous see-throughs, this shop offers chic or ethnic, classic, retro or modern styles. Designers such as Sybilla, Jean-Paul Gaultier, Marcel Marougiu, Jean Colonna, Yamamoto and Vivienne Westwood are here to give you an unusual and glamorous new look.

Zara

Avinguda del Portal de l'Angel, 24
☎ 93 301 29 25
Metro Catalunya
Avinguda Diagonal, 584
☎ 93 414 29 46
Metro Diagonal
C. Pelai, 58
☎ 93 301 09 78
Metro Catalunya
Rambla de Catalunya, 67
☎ 93 487 08 18
Metro Passeig de Gràcia
Open Mon.-Sat. 10am-9pm.

Zara is the latest brand of Spanish clothes. Its popular

range of men's, women's and children's lines are inexpensive versions of the latest looks on the high street and are made in good quality fabrics. In a pale wood setting, and with styles ranging from basic to trendy, you'll find sweaters from about €30 and summer suits for €96.

Cristina Castañer

Carrer del Mestre Nicolau, 23
☎ 93 414 24 28
Open Mon.-Sat. 10.30am-2.30pm, 4.30-8pm
Closed Sun.

Cristina has inherited the house of Castañer, famous for many years for the quality and design of its traditional espadrilles. She launches two new lines each year – in summer her range

features cotton and jute espadrilles in unusual shapes, styles and colors and in winter the collection boasts shoes made from leather with a "1950s revisited" feel.

Hipòtesi

Rambla de Catalunya, 105
☎ 93 215 02 98
Metro Passeig de Gràcia
Open Mon. & Sat. 10am-1.30pm, 5-8.30pm, Tue.-Fri. 10am-8.30pm.

Even the window display is a little gem in this jewelry shop, which sets itself apart from others with its innovative collection of pieces in such diverse materials as ceramics, glass and fabric. If you love jewelry, it would be a real shame to miss it.

Rafa Teja Atelier

C. de Santa Maria, 18
☎ 93 310 27 85
C. del Comte de Salvatierra, 10
☎ 93 237 70 59
Open Mon.-Fri. 10am-2pm, 4.30-8.30pm, Sat. 10am-2pm.

The designs in this shop combine contemporary design and handmade quality, with beautiful scarves made of natural fabrics such as silk, cotton and wool. Hand-painted and embroidered in India, they are available in a wonderful range of colors and materials.

ROSER Y FRANCESC

Carrer de València, 285
☎ 93 459 14 53
Metro Passeig de Gràcia or Diagonal
Open Mon.-Sat. 10am-2pm, 4.30-8.30pm.

There's an intimate atmosphere and a retro feel to this spot, in stark contrast to the modern clothes. You'll receive a warm welcome before you browse through local and international designs by Antonio Miró, Josep Abril, Ailanto Kenzo, Tara Jarmon and Locking Shockings.

Men's fashion

Men's fashion in Barcelona comes in every possible shape and form. Whatever style you go for – formal or casual, classic or trendy, intellectual or sporty, Latin lover or cool dude – you'll find clothes to suit you in this selection of shops.

Adolfo Dominguez

Passeig de Gràcia, 32
☎ 93 487 41 70
Passeig de Gràcia, 89
☎ 93 215 13 39
Avinguda Diagonal, 490
☎ 93 416 11 92
Open Mon.-Sat. 10am-8pm.

If you're planning a business meeting or romantic dinner with the woman in your life, the collections of this internationally famous designer are absolutely not to be missed. High-quality fabrics and natural colors give Dominguez' refined clothes a sober elegance.

David Valls

C. de València, 235
☎ 93 487 12 85
Open Mon.-Sat. 10am-2pm, 5-8.30pm.

David Valls experiments and innovates and like most of his creative contemporaries in Barcelona, he uses different fabrics (wool, silk and cotton) in a very personal way. His originality lies in the textures he achieves using the latest technology. The cuts are simple, elegant and comfortable for those wanting a "Bohemian Chic" look.

El Transwaal

C. de l'Hospital, 67
☎ 93 301 91 18
Metro Liceu
Open Mon.-Sat. 9.30am-2pm, 4.30-8pm.
A shop that's worth the visit for the sign alone. A shopwindow dummy in a starched hat welcomes you to a world of professional uniforms, including a waiter's dinner suit and chef's outfit. Ideal for impressing the guests at your next dinner party.

Camper

Centre Commercial el Triangle
C. de Pelai 13-37
☎ 93 302 41 24
Open Mon.-Sat. 10.30am-10pm.

In the newly built shopping center in the Plaça de Catalunya, you'll get off on the right foot with Camper's crepe soles and colorful supple leathers. You'll find innovative shoe designs for everyone.

Furest

Avinguda Diagonal, 468
☎ 93 416 06 65
Passeig de Gràcia, 12-14
☎ 93 301 20 00
Open Mon.-Sat. 10am-2pm, 4.30-8pm.

This temple to sartorial elegance has been selling classic designs for men for many generations. Clothes range from tailored suits to casual and sportswear, and the collections are sophisticated and top quality.

Gonzalo Comella

Avinguda Diagonal, 478
☎ 93 416 15 16
Metro Diagonal
Open Mon.-Sat. 10am-8.30pm.
Passeig de Gràcia, 6
☎ 93 412 66 00
Metro Catalunya
Open Mon.-Sat. 10am-9pm.

You'll find fashionable clothes for both town and country, including parkas by Antonio Miró, Ralph Lauren pullovers, Hugo Boss suits, Armani shirts and Church's shoes.

Tribu

C. Avinyó, 12
☎ 93 318 65 10
Metro Liceu
Open Mon.-Sat. 10am-2pm, 4.30-8.30pm.

In one of the city's most fashionable streets, this new boutique has been the object of so much hype that it now attracts all of Barcelona's trendy crowd. Dresses cut out of parachute fabric, hand-painted, customized polo shirts and vintage Diesel, are all displayed around installations by the latest artists. Tribu is where you want to be seen!

Sombreria Obach

C. del Call, 2
☎ 93 318 40 94
Metro Liceu
Open Mon.-Fri. 9.30am-1.30pm, 4-8pm, Sat. 4.30-8pm.

In the heart of the old town, Sombreria Obach have been making hats for three generations. Take your pick from caps (€6-24), Basque berets (*boinas,* €12), *barretina catalana* – Catalan caps that are worn pulled down over one ear (€5.40) – and light straw panamas (€36-66) for the look that suits you best.

UMBRELLAS FOR ALL...JULIO GOMEZ

Las Ramblas, 104
☎ 93 412 72 58
Metro Liceu
Open Mon.-Sat. 9am-1.30pm, 4-8pm.

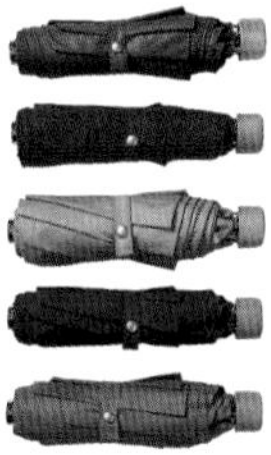

This is one of the oldest businesses on the Ramblas. Since 1865, the people of Barcelona having been coming here to have umbrella ribs and walking-sticks repaired. Buy a *baston* (walking stick, €2.40-72) and make a grand entrance at the Liceu theater. The stars of musical comedies and even Gene Kelly placed orders here, so why not you?

Children's clothes and games

In a country with one of the lowest birth rates in Europe, it isn't surprising that children are treated like royalty. Like the Italians, the Spanish have always loved children and you will find that they are readily accepted in most places. Here are some suggestions for places to spoil your own.

El Rey de la Magia

C. de la Princesa, 11
☎ 93 319 39 20
Metro Jaume I
Open Mon.-Fri. 10am-2pm, 5-8pm (closed Sat. pm).

Everything for children who want to be magicians when they grow up. Jokes and tricks of every kind, including conjuring tricks and sleight-of-hand that are just the thing for the budding magician. With a blood-red shopwindow display and a sign in the form of a turbaned genie with a hypnotic stare, be prepared to fall under its spell.

Juguetes Foyé

C. dels Banys Nous, 13
☎ 93 302 03 89
Metro Liceu
Open Mon.-Fri. 10am-2pm, 4.30-8pm, Sat. 5-8pm.

Four generations of the Foyé family have kept the children of Barcelona happy over the years in this, the oldest toy shop in the city. There are metal toys for collectors and model horses in papier mâché (€72), musical boxes (€84), steam engines and fancy dress.

Drap

C. del Pi, 14
☎ 93 318 14 87
Metro Liceu
Open Mon.-Sat. 9.30am-1.30pm, 4.30-8.30pm.

Few little girls will be able to resist these delightful doll's houses. Palaces, chalets and two-story Victorian houses cost €240-2,400. Don't forget that once your dream house has been chosen, its walls have to be papered, fire-places have to be installed, curtains hung and finally it has to be furnished. Quite an expensive business!

Rosès

Avinguda del Portal de l'Angel, 15
☎ 93 302 03 34
Metro Catalunya
Open Mon.-Fri. 9.45am-1.30pm, 4.30-8pm, Sat. 10.15am-2pm.

In a street where an angel is supposed to have once appeared, it isn't surprising to

find a shop selling *figuras para belenes* (crib figures). The traditional cribs of Murcia and Olot (€36) always include a fertility symbol, the *caganer*, as described on p. 14.

Kiddy's Class

Via Augusta, 45
☎ 93 237 96 12
Metro Diagonal
Open Mon.-Sat. 10am-8.30pm.

A great choice of clothes at unbeatable prices. Good value sportswear with a hint of the traditional and a touch of the classroom. Shirts around €16, T-shirts €9 and dresses €24.

Sardina Submarina

C. del Cardenal Casañas, 7
☎ 93 317 11 79
Open Mon.-Sat. 10am-2pm, 5-8.30pm

This colorful shop behind the Ramblas mainly specializes in wooden toys – scooters, cookery utensils and tea sets, puppets and Danish mobiles – as well as board games and lamps for all ages.

Oilily

C. del Tenor Viñas, 1
☎ 93 201 84 79
Ferrocarril Muntaner
Open Mon.-Sat. 10.15am-2pm, 4.30-8.15pm.
A riot of color and pretty prints will add a cheerful note to your children's wardrobes, with attractive little floral skirts, checked lumberjack shirts, Sioux-Indian-style sweaters, and exclusive bikinis and swimwear. The prices, however, can be a little on the high side.

Imaginarium

Rambla de Catalunya, 31
Metro Catalunya
Moll d'Espanya, Maremagnum
Metro Drassanes
☎ 93 225 80 50
Open Mon.-Sat. 10am-8.30pm.

A colorful and brightly lit setting for open-air games – trampolines, slides, swings and inflatable swimming pools. And if you can't imagine

where you'd put it all, you can choose from the smaller toys such as skittles, rocking horses, spinning-tops and drums.

Menkes

Gran Via de les Corts Catalanes, 642
☎ 93 318 86 47
Metro Passeig de Gràcia
Open Mon.-Sat. 10am-1.30pm, 5-8.30pm.

Founded in 1950, Menkes is the place to go for fancy dress costumes, such as Sleeping Beauty, a toreador or a flamenco dancer – with or without false eyelashes (€66 to €90). It's an incredible Aladdin's Cave, where children can find just the outfit they want to really make an impression at a fancy dress party back home.

EL INGENIO

C. d'En Rauric, 6
☎ 93 317 71 38. Metro Liceu
Open Mon.-Sat. 10am-1.30pm, 4.15-8pm.

El Ingenio is a shop with a carnival atmosphere. Since 1838, the Cardona family have been making masks and *cap-grossos*, the giants' heads that parade through the streets of Barcelona and Sitges. You can see a workshop at the back where the unfinished papier-mâché heads have something very bizarre and surreal about them. Even Dalí was fascinated by this highly unusual place.

Department stores and shopping arcades

Shops are usually open until around 7.30 or 8pm during the week and 6pm is a particularly busy time as people shop after work. However, don't forget that a few stores close for *siesta* after lunch (usually between 2 and 4.30pm), so don't expect all the shops to be open then. The newest stores and arcades, Maremagnum and Illà, have striking window displays, a source of great pride to the people of Barcelona.

El Corte Inglés

Plaça de Catalunya, 14
☎ 93 306 38 00

Metro Catalunya
Avinguda Diagonal, 617
☎ 93 419 28 28
Metro Maria Cristina
Open Mon.-Sat. 10am-10pm.

This famous department store stands in the Plaça de Catalunya like a vast Art-Deco ocean liner. It's the city's biggest store and stocks a wide range of goods. However, be warned, prices are rather high and the ladies' fashion department is a little on the staid side. Still, if you can't find anything you like, you can always enjoy the view from the restaurant.

Maremagnum

Moll d'Espanya
☎ 93 225 81 00
Metro Drassanes
Open Mon.-Sun. 11am-11pm.

The most recent addition to the city's shore area and the

pride of the people of Barcelona, this vast shopping center has become an obligatory part of the Sunday stroll, with its mixture of cafés, restaurants, bars and shops. Maremagnum caters for all tastes, from the high-tech and kitsch to the eco-friendly and green. It's a bold construction of glass panels and wooden walkways, with a good view of the harbor.

Bulevard Rosa

Passeig de Gràcia, 55
☎ 93 215 83 31
Metro Plaça de Gràcia
Avinguda Diagonal, 474
☎ 93 215 83 31
Metro Diagonal
Open Mon.-Sat. 10.30am-8.30pm.

Hoping to find strength in numbers, the first shopping centers flourished in Barcelona, as in London, in the 1970s. There are over a

hundred shops at these Bulevard Rosa locations. The fashion, shoe, jewelry and perfume boutiques and stores, along with cafés and bars make them favorite meeting places on Friday nights for teenagers and young

professionals. The selection of shops tends to be fairly trendy and includes Marcel's, one of the "in" places to have a haircut in Barcelona (a cut costs around €30 at the Avinguda Diagonal branch).

L'Illà

Avinguda Diagonal, 557
☎ 93 444 00 00
Metro Maria Cristina
Open Mon.-Sat. 10am-9.30pm.

Located in the business district, on the Avinguda Diagonal, the three floors of this new shopping center cater to the needs of the local office workers. You'll find many of the same shops that are in Maremagnum (see opposite) are also here, as well as Marks & Spencer and the Caprabo supermarket which sells food. It's not all that exotic for the visitor, but it's extremely practical for the locals due to its strategic location and large underground parking lot.

El Triangle

Carrer de Pelai, 39
☎ 93 318 01 08
Metro Universitat
Open Mon.-Sat. 10am-9.30pm (winter), 10am-10pm (summer).

The inauguration of this huge megastore, located right in the heart of the city, put an end to the derogatory nickname by which the area had become known – the "block of shame." It sells books, clothes and CDs late into the evening and you'll find a good selection of international labels, including Habitat, Dockers, Camper and Agatha.

NO NEED TO WORRY ABOUT THE DEMISE OF THE LOCAL SHOP!

Like all cities, Barcelona suffers from the "shopping center" syndrome, yet Spaniards still prefer their traditional markets, and the city has no less than 41 covered markets. The community spirit and various commercial groups combine to produce a network of resistance across the city and small retailers courageously fend off attacks from the big boys.

Sports goods and gadgets

The people of Barcelona take part in aquatic and mountain sports with equal enthusiasm. They're fanatical about football and balconies are decked with flags in the Barça colors during the football season. If you are particularly interested in sports goods and gadgets, you will find plenty of choice here. In fact Barcelona had a very wide choice long before the Olympic Games came to town in 1992.

Sports Goods

La Botiga del Barça

Maremagnum, L27
Moll d'Espanya
☎ 93 225 80 45
Metro Barceloneta
Open Mon.-Sun. 11am-10pm.

For ardent supporters of the local football team, you'll find football shirts, shorts, flags, caps, ashtrays and key rings in the Barça colors (red and blue). You can also visit the Camp Nou Stadium and museum (see p. 19) for that total Barcelona football experience.

Jonas

Carrer de Salvador Espriu, L56-57
☎ 93 225 15 68
Metro Ciutadella Vila Olímpica
Open Mon.-Sun. 10am-10.30pm, Sat. 10am-11pm.

A red-chrome Harley Davidson in the entrance sets the tone and you know this is a shop for real enthusiasts. Jonas

specializes in extreme sports and you can get your snowboarding and surfing gear here, made of either fleece or light nylon – so, choose waves or moguls according to your mood.

Quera

C. de Petritxol, 2
☎ 93 318 07 43
Metro Liceu
Open Mon.-Fri. 9.30am-1.30pm, 4.30-8pm, Sat. 10am-1.30pm, 5-8pm.

Leaf your way through a vast array of old maps and dusty tomes in this bookshop to discover interesting routes for your trekking expedition in the Pyrenees, or elsewhere. Familiarize yourself with rock climbing, potholing or more gentle pursuits – the adventure starts here.

Gadgets

Items d'Ho

C. de Mallorca, 251
☎ 93 488 32 37
Open Mon.-Sat. 10am-8.30pm
Passeig de Gràcia, 55
Bd Rosa
☎ 93 216 09 41
Open Mon.-Fri. 10am-8.30pm, Sat. 10am-3pm, 4-8.30pm.

This shop specializes in gifts for men. From key rings and luggage to fashionable glasses cases and chromium-plated watches, everything has been carefully designed to please your "hombre."

Natura

Maremagnum, Moll d'Espanya
☎ 93 225 80 49
Metro Barceloneta
Open Mon-Sun. 11am-11pm.
Consell de Cent, 304
☎ 93 488 19 72
Open Mon.-Sat. 10am-8.30pm.

For fans of environmentally friendly design, there are wood and rattan lamps, Mexican mobiles (€2.94), candle holders, Afghan hats and T-shirts defending the rights of the whale – a little touch of Greenpeace – wrapped in recycled paper.

Dom

C. Provença, 249
☎ 93 487 11 81
Metro Diagonal Carrer Avinyó, 7
☎ 93 342 55 91
Open Mon.-Sat. 10.30am-8.30pm.

Wacky and unusual designs such as bags made from fun fur fabrics and brightly colored nylon and pens that look like plastic flowers.

D Barcelona

Avinguda Diagonal, 367
☎93 216 03 46
Metro Passeig de Gràcia
Open Mon.-Sat.10.30am-2pm, 4.30-9pm.
Maremagnum, local 39
☎ 93 225 80 86
Open Mon.-Sat. 11am-11pm.

An unusual shop packed with kitsch, practical, funny or zany gadgets, including sheepskin photo frames, fluorescent shower curtains and genuine leatherette sofas. Definitely just for fun.

COLONEL TAPIOCA

Portal de l'Angel, 4
☎ 93 318 20 35
Metro Catalunya
Open Mon.-Fri. 10am-8.30pm, Sat. 11am-10pm.

The *Raiders of the Lost Ark* must have got their gear here. If you fancy going on a safari, camel expedition, jeep rally or just like the "Out of Africa" look, come along to the Colonel's and he'll supply you with everything you need. From the penknife to the survival kit, by way of the portable solar stove, you won't be short of anything next time you leave.

Decoration,
tableware and design

Barcelona is reputed for being at the forefront of innovative contemporary design, so capitalize on your weekend by acquiring a designer piece for your home. If you have very eclectic tastes, you won't be disappointed by what's on offer. Colonial, country, high-tech, kitsch, utility, unusual or surrealist, there are as many styles as there are shops.

Molsa

Plaça San Josep Oriol, 1
☎ 93 302 31 03
Metro Liceu
Open Mon.-Sat. 10am-8pm.

At the foot of the Santa Maria del Pi church steeple, Molsa has an authentic range of Spanish craft objects on display – traditional ceramics from Galicia and Valencia, glassware from Mallorca, blue-and-white checked window boxes, reproductions of 18th-century Catalan tableware, sundials and colorful *azulejos* (tiles).

Beardsley

C. de Petritxol, 12
☎ 93 301 05 76

Metro Liceu
Open Mon.-Sat. 10am-2pm, 4.30-8pm.

A shop window with an air of home-sweet-home about it, in this small lively street. Beardsley sells pot-pourri, dried flowers, petit-point embroidery, needlework, white Girona porcelain, bathroom accessories and, in the basement, a colorful range of cardboard storage boxes (€120-24), in flowery and checked designs and personalized writing paper (€3.58).

Punto Luz

C. de Pau Claris, 146
☎ 93 216 03 93
Metro Passeig de Gràcia
Open Mon.-Fri. 9.30am-1.30pm 4.30-8pm, Sat. 10am-1.30pm, 5-8pm.

There's no need to be kept in the dark, as you'll find a sophisticated selection of lighting that will appeal to even the most demanding tastes. Say goodbye to those dreary old lampshades and dull colors. There are also lights and shades for the garden. Everything is bang up-to-the minute and fashionable.

Again

C. del Palau, 6
☎ 93 301 54 52
Metro Liceu or Jaume 1
Open Mon.-Sat. 10am-2pm, 4.30-8pm.

Fashions come and go, and come back again! This is where the 1970's have made their comeback in Barcelona, in this tiny street of the Barrio Gótico district. From the fake leather sofas to the spherical stainless steel lamps, the bright red bathroom shelves and the canary yellow ashtrays, this shop pays homage to the era of plastic, fakes and flower power.

Juan Soriano Raura

Mayor de Gràcia, 53
☎ 93 217 23 75
Open Mon.-Sat. 9am-2pm, 4.30-8pm.

When you leave the Passeig de Gràcia, make for this cut-price hardware shop. Dating from the 1890s, it's an Aladdin's Cave full of amazing bric-a-brac. Every item comes with detailed instructions for use and you're bound to find something you like amid the jumble that includes paella dishes, ramekins for *crema catalana* and *porronés,* which you drink from without letting the bottle touch your lips. A real curiosity shop.

Coses de Casa

Plaça San Josep Oriol, 5
☎ 93 302 7
Metro Liceu
Open Mon-Sat. 9am-2pm, 4.30-8pm.

If you have a strong liking for Catalan design, then this is the place for you. In these antiquated surroundings you'll find a unique selection of Catalan fabrics, including the distinctive *llengos de Mallorca* (see box below) in striking reds, blues and greens, with more in shades of golden yellow and coral pink.

Entre Telas

Plaça Vicenç Martorell, 1
☎ 93 317 76 14
Open Mon.-Sat. 10am-2pm, 5-8pm.

This textile workshop has taken up lodgings under the arcades of a shady square in the Raval district, where two young designers happily produce a blend of craft and design. Hand-woven silk and cotton tinted with vegetable dyes are printed with exclusive, personalized designs. They're said to have "good vibrations," so go ahead and treat yourself.

TRADITIONAL TEXTILES

Catalonia has an ancient textile tradition, and the Balearic Islands, and Mallorca in particular, have preserved the old weaving skills. At Santa Maria del Cami there is one manufacturer still producing the famous *llengos de Mallorca*. The cloth, half cotton and half linen, is 70cm/27in wide. The most typical pattern is the *raxa*. This stiff, rough cloth mixes shades of indigo, blue, coral pink, green and golden yellow to striking effect (around €21-24 per meter).

Caixa de Fang

C. de Freneria, 1
☎ 93 315 17 04
Metro Jaume I
Open Mon.-Sat. 10am-2pm, 4-8pm.

Behind the cathedral, gourmets will find all the utensils they need to concoct tasty Catalan dishes – salamander irons (€3.76), ramekins for *crema catalana*, *porronés*, for drinking without letting your lips touch the bottle, terra-cotta cooking pots, glazed ceramics and boxwood and olive-wood spoons (€0.75-1.95).

Servicio Estaciòn

C. d'Aragó, 270-272
☎ 93 216 02 12
Metro Passeig de Gràcia
Open Mon.-Fri. 9.30am-2pm, 4.15-8pm, Sat. 9.45am-2pm, 4.30-8.15pm.

A gigantic hardware shop, where you'll find waxed cloth and plastic and Formica kitchen tiles. If you're looking for paella dishes (see p. 11), also try Juan Soriano Raura (see p. 111).

Taller de Lenceria

C. de Rosselló, 271
☎ 93 451 39 52
Metro Diagonal
Open Mon.-Sat. 10am-2pm, 4.30-8pm.

Elegant table and bed linen made to measure in cotton, linen and lace, as well as a large selection of cotton piqué nightdresses and pyjamas on which you can have your initials embroidered.

Sit Down

C. de Mallorca, 331
☎ 93 207 75 32
Metro Verdaguer
Open Mon.-Sat. 10am-1.30pm, 4.30-8pm.

You'll be spoiled for choice between re-issues of natural cane chairs by Oscar Tusquets and other designs by Joseph Hoffmann, Philippe Starck and Jose Luis Luscà, making good use of color and fabric and all reasonably priced.

LOVE AT FIRST SITE

Coral Bells Oficis
C. de la Palla,15
☎ 93 412 16 68
Metro Liceu
Open Mon.-Fri. 10.30am-1.30pm, 4-8pm, Sat. 10.30am-1.30pm, 5-8pm.

Cut-crystal glasses, Murano vases, intricately designed porcelain cups decorated with gold leaf, lacquered bowls, fine crystal sculptures, books made of cotton: you step into this shop as if in a waking dream. Carme Coral has the knack for picking only the very best artists, craftsmen and designers, from Catalonia and beyond, to exhibit their work in this narrow street in the heart of Barcelona.

Tierra Extraña

C. de Rosselló, 226
☎ 93 487 95 88
Open Mon.-Sat. 10.30am-8.30pm.

As the name suggests, you're on foreign soil here, with Indonesian and colonial Indian furniture, parchment wall-lamps (€78), palm basketwork and craft objects displayed on low rattan tables that will make you believe you're in tropical climes.

Pilma

Avinguda Diagonal, 403
☎ 93 416 13 99
Metro Diagonal
Open Mon.-Sat. 10am-2pm, 4.30-8.30pm.

Modern lifestyle in a contemporary transparent steel and glass setting. On the ground floor you'll find kitchen and bathroom accessories, on the first floor there's a passageway

leading to a loggia full of light, colorful furniture. From pure wool tartan plaid fabrics to futuristic baskets, by way of the Noguchi paper lantern, Pilma clearly has plenty to offer.

Hammam

C. dels Flassaders, 42
☎ 93 268 32 39
Metro Jaume I
Open Mon.-Sat. 11am-2pm, 4.30-8pm (Sat. until 9pm).

Kitsch is back and you can find it at Hammam. Or, if you prefer, there's also a wide range of "Peace and Love" and other 1970s-style items. Futons, artificial flowers, leopardskin lampshades, subdued lighting – that little bit of fun and of course bags of atmosphere. Friendly and amusing.

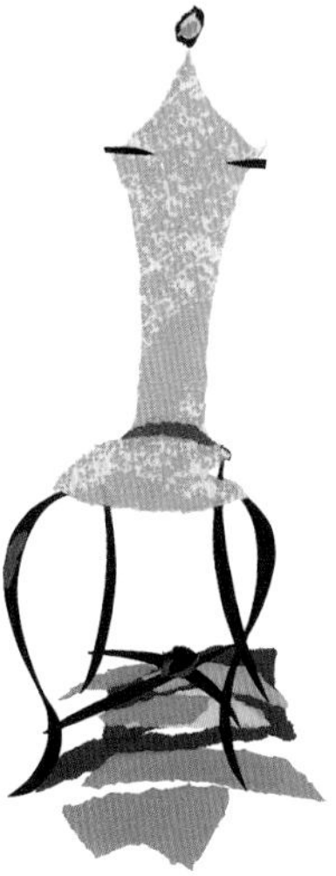

Arkitektura

Via Augusta, 185
☎ 93 362 47 20
Ⓕ 93 241 17 85
Open Mon.-Fri. 9.30am-2pm, 4-7.30pm, Sat. 10am-2pm.

This new space is dedicated to contemporary design for the home and office. In the large showroom you'll find a careful selection of the best of today's design. Arkitektura's mission is to marry avant-garde design with aesthetic appeal and a high degree of functionality. You'll find examples of furniture by all the latest designers – Alias, Armani, Depadova, Tecno and Azucena.

NOT FORGETTING...

Your visit would not be complete without seeing some of the design classics of yesterday and today. Try the **BD** boutique (Mallorca, 291) and **Vinçon** and **Tinçon**, sister shops found in Pg. de Gràcia, 96 and C. de Rosselló, 246, respectively (☎ 93 215 60 50, open Mon.-Sat. 10am-2pm, 4.30-8.30pm) where you'll find a huge range of original and modern objects for the home. Also try their website: www.vincon.com.

Antiques shops and flea markets

From the bric-a-brac of an antiques dealer to the open-air secondhand stalls in the Plaça del Pi, you'll discover the pleasures of bargain-hunting in the sun. You may not find the bargain of the century, but don't let that stop you bringing back something to remind you of Barcelona and the warm Mediterranean when you get back home.

Els Encants

Plaça de las Glòries
☎ 93 246 30 30
Metro Glòries
Open Mon., Wed., Fri. and Sat. 9am-5.30pm in winter, 9am-6pm (or 7pm) in summer.

The name "Encant" comes from *cantar* (singing), as merchants here used to sing out the prices. Els Encants is a cross between a scrap metal yard and a jumble sale. There are bicycle wheels, books, old sofas, buttons, lamps – you name it, someone at Els Encants will be selling it. A real flea market in the sun, but you'll need to get up early for the best finds.

El Bulevard dels Antiquaris

Passeig de Gràcia, 55
☎ 93 215 44 99
Metro Passeig de Gràcia
Open Mon.-Sat. 9.30am-8.30pm.

In an elegant shopping center in the Passeig, art lovers and collectors will find a clutch of good quality antique shops. It's a chance to take a quick look at a wide selection of quality items.

Mercat Gotic

Avinguda Catedral, 6
☎ 93 291 61 18
Metro Liceu.

Every Thursday from 9am-8pm (except in August), secondhand stalls set up shop in the cathedral square. Search hard and you may find some pretty *azulejos*, old ceramics, a doll with porcelain eyes, or carved whale teeth. Bric-a-brac with soul.

Mercat Sant Antoni

C. del Comte d'Urgell, 1
☎ 93 423 42 87
Metro Sant Antoni
Clothes: open Mon., Wed., Fri. and Sat. 9am-7pm; Books: open Sun. 9am-2pm.

In an iron and glass hall dating from 1872, Sant Antoni's market is a bargain-hunter's paradise, where ladies who lunch happily rub shoulders with high-spirited teens, looking for clothes and accessories from eras before they were born. Every Sunday from 10am to 2pm, secondhand clothes change hands, and old editions of Tintin in Catalan, faded posters, color prints and film magazines all vie for the favors of keen collectors. In one corner, they swap the latest characters from Japanese role playing games. There's something to suit all tastes here.

La Inmaculada Concepcion

C. de Rosselló, 271
☎ 93 217 78 90
Metro Diagonal
Open Mon.-Sat. 10am-2pm, 4.30-8pm.

One of the pioneers of recycled furniture – *Modernista*, industrial and American-style office furniture – and also the designer of lamps with parchment lampshades.

Josep Pascual i Armengou

Carrer dels Banys Nous, 14
☎ 93 301 53 65
Open Mon.-Sat. lunchtime 11am-1.30pm, 5-8pm.

The Banys Nous and Paja streets (Metro Liceu), in the heart of the old town, are crammed with interesting shops. Enter the maze and wander around to your heart's content. At Josep Pascual i Armengou you'll find early Catalan furniture, chests and *azulejo* tiles.

Gotham

C. de Cervantes, 7
☎ 93 412 46 47
Open Mon.-Sat. 10.30am-2pm, 5-8.30pm.

A shop decorated in acid colors and translucent plastic, selling furniture from the 1950s to 1970s to brighten up your world. Better than a course of vitamins and sure to banish the blues.

Rosa Cortés Interiors

C. de Pau Claris, 183
☎ 93 215 31 45
Open Mon.-Sat. 10am-1.30pm, 5-8pm.

This is the place to come if you like antique rustic furniture. It's like stepping into the countryside with its regional artisan pieces in Catalan wrought iron and Mallorcan blown glass.

Urbana

C. de Seneca, 13
☎ 93 237 36 44
Metro Diagonal
Open Mon.-Fri. 10am-2pm, 4.30-8pm
No credit cards.

Right at the top of the passeig, in an extraordinary setting, you'll find relics salvaged from Spanish town houses (fireplaces from €1,500, plus bathroom accessories), old cinema seats, Chirico-style shop dummies, old shop signs and decorations. At Carrer de Còrsega, 258 you'll find Urbana, a shop specializing in old fireplaces.

BARGAIN-HUNTING

The feature spread "Antiques and old lace" (see pp. 20-21), gives details of some sought after items and where to look for them. For more information contact:

Erika Niedermaier
C. de la Palla, 11
☎ 93 412 79 24
Mon.-Sat 10.30am-1.30pm, 4.15-8pm, Sat 11am-1.30pm.

Maria Jose Royo
C. Banys Nous, 22
Tienda 1
☎ 93 302 35 20
Mon.-Fri. 10am-1.30pm, 4.30-8pm, Sat. 11am-1.30pm.

Hobbies and collections

You don't need to be particularly wealthy to be a collector, as long as you don't decide to collect Fabergé eggs that is, and some people do collect the strangest things. However, whatever your particular interest there's nothing quite like the pleasure of adding a foreign piece to your collection while on your travels.

Monge

C. dels Boters, 2
☎ 93 317 94 35
Metro Liceu
Open Mon.-Sat. 9am-1.30pm, 4-8pm.

Philatelist or not, Monge is worth a visit for the *Modernista* shopfront alone.

Since 1904, Señor Monge has prided himself on his knowledge of coins and stamps. His collections include 1st- and 2nd-century coins, and the more affordable sets of stamps of the Olympic Games (€3).

Palau

C. de Pelai, 34
☎ 93 317 36 78
Metro Catalunya
Open Mon.-Sat. 10am-1.30pm, 4.30-8.30pm.

A firm founded in 1935 selling the Scalextric, Meccano and Fleischmann brands. Everything is on a small scale here except the cashier and the prices. Expect to pay between €156 and €409 for an electric train. Have a look at the dozens of miniature electric lights – they're just like the real thing.

Proa

C. d'Aribau, 140
☎ 93 453 16 15
Metro Diagonal
Open Mon.-Fri. 10am-2pm, 5-9pm, Sat. until 5.30pm.

The boutique for lovers of the sea – locally known as "el mar." Sit back on a boat-shaped couch and enjoy the extraordinary collection of storm lamps, lighthouse apparatus, telescopes, sextants, compasses and astronomical devices. They also have their own line of clothes. Plenty of ideas for making presents.

Norma Comics

Passeig de Sant Joan, 7
☎ 93 244 84 20
Metro Arc de Triomf
Open Mon.-Sat. 10.30am-2pm, 5-8.30pm.

Comic book collectors will find this store a good source for

first editions, while fans of role-playing games, war games and *Star Wars* aficionados can stock up on cards, dice and accessories. If none of these spark any interest in you, you can always take a look at the Japanese printing machines which are also for sale.

Sagarra

C. de la Palla, 3
☎ 93 412 59 27
Metro Liceu
Open Mon.-Sat. 10am-2pm, 4-8pm.

In this street famous for its antique dealers, near the cathedral, this small old fashioned shop generates an instant feeling of familiarity, like an old family house. Early 20th-century miniature crockery, porcelain dolls, lead figurines and antique puppet theaters. This well stored attic, run by an energetic matron, will enchant you.

L'Estanc

Via Laietana, 4
☎ 93 310 10 34
Open Mon.-Fri. 9am-2pm, 4-8pm, Sat. 10am-2pm.

If you are keen on good quality cigars you should visit this shop. The owner is a cigar *puros* (purist). He's an expert in Cuban tobacco and stocks over 150,000 cigars in his cellar. Smoking connoisseurs keep theirs locked away and meet to discuss them with other aficionados from time to time. Comfortable chairs and a glass of whisky help the conversation to flow. A box of 25 no.4 Montecristo cigars will cost you around €90.

Hobby Tècnic

C. del Comte d'Urgell, 182
☎ 93 323 39 45
Open Mon.-Sat. 9.30am-1.30pm, 4.30-8.30pm.

These models will occupy you on rainy days when you get back home. Hobby Tècnic sells top international brands of model planes, boats and trains. A technical service is also available and there are even spare parts for sale.

Mercado de Numismatica y Filatelia

Plaça Reial
Metro Liceu.

On Sunday mornings (9am-2.30pm) coin and stamp collectors gather beneath the arcades of the Plaça Reial. Regardless of whether you have a particular interest in coin and stamp collecting, this is a very colorful market and a good place for a spot of people-watching.

A NATIONAL OBSESSION!

With nearly ten draws a week, the Spanish lottery drives the country insane. Tickets can be purchased for as little as €1.50 from the tiny *venda du cupó* stalls or from the street salesmen, generally found half asleep under an umbrella. You'll come across them everywhere. The great Loteria Nacional takes place on Thursdays and Saturdays (€12 minimum). Will you join the millions of lottery addicts who every day wait anxiously for the results to be published in the papers and on TV?

The art market
and art galleries

The most important art galleries are located in Carrer del Consell de Cent (between C. de Pau Claris and C. de Balmes), while newly fashionable areas, such as the Raval or Born, are witnessing the opening of new galleries spearheading the avant-garde. The following places are both legendary and visionary, to whet your appetite.

Sala Parès

C. de Petritxol, 5
☎ 93 318 70 08
Metro Liceu
Open Mon.-Sat. 10.30am-2pm, 4.30-8.30pm, Sun. 11.30am-2pm.

The oldest art gallery in the city (1840), where the work of the great turn-of-the-last-century Catalan painters, such as Rusinol, Casas, Nonell and Picasso, was exhibited. Each Sunday morning after attending Mass, people would visit this avant-garde institution to discuss art, politics and religion. In 1928, Dalí honored it with his presence. A visit to this legendary place is essential for art lovers.

Galeria Maragall

Rambla de Catalunya, 116
☎ 93 218 29 60
Open Mon.-Fri. 10am-1.30pm, 4.30-8.30pm, Sat. 10.30am-2pm, 5.30-8.30pm.

This gallery exhibits work by Catalan artists, in particular Tàpies and Miró from the older generation of artists and the more recent Castro and Enrick. It's also a good place if you are interested in lithographs. It has a very good collection and the prices aren't unreasonable, starting at around €21.

Metronom

C. de la Fusina, 9
☎ 93 268 42 98
Metro Jaume I
Open Tue.-Sat. 10am-2pm, 4.30-8.30pm.

This is the gallery of the famous collector Rafael Tous, which flourishes in the shadow of the Born market. It also houses a contemporary art foundation which is one of the keystones of cultural life in Barcelona.

Ras

C. del Doctor Dou, 10
☎ 93 412 71 99
Email: ras@oike.com
Metro Catalunya
Open Tue.-Sat. 1-9pm.

Ras is an interesting contemporary art gallery, which hosts exhibitions and conferences on architecture, design and photography. The library is also very innovative and up-to-the-minute.

Cultural Centre of the Caixa-Palau Macaya Foundation

Passeig de Sant Joan, 108
☎ 93 476 86 00
Open Tue.-Sat. 11am-8pm, Sun. 11am-3pm.

La Caixa is the fifth-largest non-profit-making cultural institution in the world, hence its dynamism (see panel). Located in this remarkable *Modernista* palace, designed by Puig i Cadafalch, it has exhibition rooms, concert halls, reading rooms, sound archives, a video library, a book-shop and a bar.

Ediciones T

C. del Consell de Cent, 282
☎ 93 487 64 02
Metro Passeig de Gràcia
Open Tue.-Fri. 10am-2pm, 4-8pm, Sat 11am-2pm, 5-8.30pm.

Inaugurated in September 1994 by the son of Antoni Tàpies (see p. 29), this gallery specializes in original graphic works, books illustrated by artists such as Arroyo, Campano, Chullida, Le Witt and, of course, Tàpies.

Dels Ángels

C. dels Ángels, 16
☎ 93 412 54 54
Metro Catalunya
Open Tue.-Sat. noon-2pm, 5-8.30pm.

Galleries flourish in the restored area of the Raval, thanks to the Museum of Contemporary Art, which helps young experimental artists to become established. A drawing by Santi Moix, for example, costs around €270, while paintings range from €901-€3,125. A great place to spot new trends.

LA CAIXA, NOT JUST A SAVINGS BANK

Since 1990, La Caixa (pronounce the Catalan "x" like the English "sh") has become the second-most powerful banking body in Spain. Omnipresent in the Arts and Sciences, it has revived the turn-of-the-last-century tradition of patronage. Its five-pointed blue star logo, designed by Miró, hovers over the whole city, a symbol of the economic and cultural power of Catalonia.

Craft and ecology

In Barcelona, as in many of the big cities of the world, people are hankering to return to a simpler way of life and are concerned with conserving the resources of the planet. In keeping with this you can now buy *organicas*, shirts made from Peruvian cotton, and *tortillas paisanas*, made of wheat. If you are into a "green" lifestyle, you can pursue it in Barcelona just as well as in London or New York.

Hôma

C. del Rec, 20
☎ 93 315 27 55
Metro Jaume I
Open Tue.-Fri. 5-9pm, Sat. 11am-2pm, 5-9pm.

A former coffee warehouse in the Ribera has been converted into a very pleasant exhibition hall, with bedside lamps and exclusive eco-friendly wall lights in a primitive style, made of natural materials – raffia, wood and bamboo. The furniture by Ruben Vidal will add a "recycled" touch to your home.

Indian

Passatge de Mercader, 16
☎ 93 487 37 03
Metro Verdaguer
Open Mon.-Sat. 10.30am-2pm, 5-8.30pm.

Faience, delicate *azulejo* (tile) patterns created in the time-honored way, embroidery, handmade carpets, traditional fabrics, Indian rice measures and colonial furniture. Those who appreciate a blend of cultures should come to Indian.

Arunachala

C. de Jovellanos, 1
☎ 93 317 80 23
Metro Catalunya
Open Mon.-Fri. 9.30am-2pm, 4.30-8.30pm, Sat. 10.30am-2pm, 5-8pm.

This bookshop, a short walk from the Plaça de Catalunya specializes in the mysteries of the occult sciences, from Zen Buddhism to reincarnation and the New Age. There is a heady smell of incense in the air, which may encourage you to have your palm read and find out about your love life.

Dauer

C. dels Tallers, 48 bis
☎ 93 318 22 41
Metro Catalunya
Open Mon.-Fri. 10am-1.30pm, 4.30-8.30pm, Sat. 10am-1.30pm, 5-8.30pm.

The walls of this shop are lined

with aquariums full of colorful fish. They specialize in piranhas, sea horses and other marine and freshwater creatures here. Pay a visit if you're feeling a bit stressed by the bustle of the streets outside and see if watching fish will have the required calming effect. Its a bit tricky to take a fish home with you, but if you feel so inclined, they range in price between €1.20 and €120.

The Living Stone

C. de Petritxol, 4
☎ 93 318 35 67
Metro Liceu
Open Mon.-Fri. 10.30am-1.30pm, 5-8.30pm, Sat. 10.30am-2pm, 4.30-8.30pm.

This warm, sun-filled shop sells a range of eco-friendly cosmetics perfumed with the scents of the Spanish countryside and the Orient.

The fragrances of bergamot, musk, honey, jasmine and patchouli fill the glass bottles.

Cereria Subirà

Baixada de la Llibreteria, 7
☎ 93 315 26 06
Metro Jaume I
Open Mon.-Sat. 9am-1.30pm, 4-7.30pm (closed Sat. pm).

In 1909, one of the city's oldest firms of candlemakers moved into this building constructed in 1847. Gilded paneling, two classic statues and an elegant staircase give it a timeless feel. Salvador Dalí often used to come here, drawn by the old-fashioned atmosphere. The owner of Cereria Subirà is understandably proud of his hand-finished, natural beeswax candles.

Herbolari Antiga Casa Guarro

C. d'En Xuclà, 23
☎ 93 301 14 44
Metro Catalunya
Open Mon.-Fri. 9am-2pm, 4-8pm, Sat. 9am-2pm, 5-8pm.

If conventional medicines no longer have the required effect on your ailments, you can rediscover some age-old herbal remedies here. Also visit the natural products fair In the Plaça de Saint Josep, the first Friday and Saturday of every month.

ATTITUDES TO SMOKING

The Spanish smoke a great deal and there are very few restrictions – in shops, in the metro, even in restaurants there are virtually no "No Smoking" areas either. If you are a smoker try going to **Gimeno**, Passeig De Gràcia, 101, open 10am-1.30pm, 4-8pm every day except Sunday. You can sit in a comfortable armchair and have a choice of pipe or cigarette holder and a lighter. Smoking at Gimeno is seen as a virtue rather than a sin, you won't find you're banished to the bottom of the garden when you need a puff.

Bookshops and stationery

Of all the countries in Europe, the Spanish read the least number of books per head. Yet Barcelona is traditionally associated with novels and art-book publishing; the city has five monuments dedicated to books, and books are given as gifts on Sant Jordi's Day (see p. 15).

Llibreria del Raval

Carrer d'Elisabets, 6
☎ 93 317 02 93
Metro Catalunya
Open Mon.-Fri. 10am-8.30pm, Sat. 10am-2.30pm, 5-8.30pm.

This bookshop is located in the sanctuary of a former chapel, behind the new Museum of Contemporary Art. It resembles a vast library on whose shelves you can find almost anything and everything from large format art books, comic strip books and novels to more esoteric works.

Continuarà

Via Laietana, 29
☎ 93 310 43 52
Metro Jaume I
Open Mon.-Sat. 10.30am-3pm, 4-9pm.

Here you'll find two floors that are home to every kind of comic strip book you can imagine. The first floor is devoted to the more modern heroes, while the one below specializes in the old favorites such as Zorro, Spiderman and Superman, who, despite being 80 years old, are just as agile as ever.

Estilografica

C. de Fontanella, 17
☎ 93 318 64 95
Metro Catalunya
Open Mon.-Sat. 9am-1.30pm, 4-8pm.

Founded in 1938, this shop has a fine selection of pens, biros and pen holders, *unica en precios y calidad*, as well as a workshop for repairs. Despite email, letter-writing lives on.

Papirum

Baixada de la Llibreteria, 2
Metro Jaume I
Open Mon.-Fri. 10am-8.30pm, Sat. 10am-2pm, 5-8.30pm.

This small shop lit by a porcelain lamp contains some fine paper craft items made locally – seals, handmade paper, boxes and diaries all lined with iridescent marbled paper. These items are exclusive to Papirum and are absolutely unique in the city (from €3-42).

La Central

C. de Mallorca, 237
☎ 93 487 50 18
Metro Passeig de Gràcia
Open Mon.-Sat. 10am-9pm (closed Sun.).
Located in a lovely apartment in the city center, this international bookshop is dedicated to those interested in the humanities. It has a welcoming and intimate atmosphere and is a perfect spot for immersing yourself in works of literature, history, sociology, anthropology, philosophy, cinema and art (in several languages).

Tarlatana

C. de la Comtessa de Sobradiel, 2
☎ 93 310 36 25
Metro Jaume I
Open Mon.-Fri. 9.30am-7pm.
In the Barrio Gótico, Jaume Salvado has perfected the art of bookbinding and framing in the traditional way. The workshop upstairs is worth looking round. Tarlatana also has a selection of pens, diaries, blotters and colored paper.

Llibreria Rodes

Carrer dels Banys Nous, 8
☎ 93 318 13 89
Open Mon.-Fri. 10am-2pm, 4-8pm (call on Sat. before visiting).

The tone is set as soon as you cross the threshold. From floor to ceiling, walls are lined with old works, out-of-print books and 18th-century engravings. A cat purrs happily in the corner and the atmosphere is calm and hushed. It's entirely fitting for a bookshop set in the heart of the antiques district.

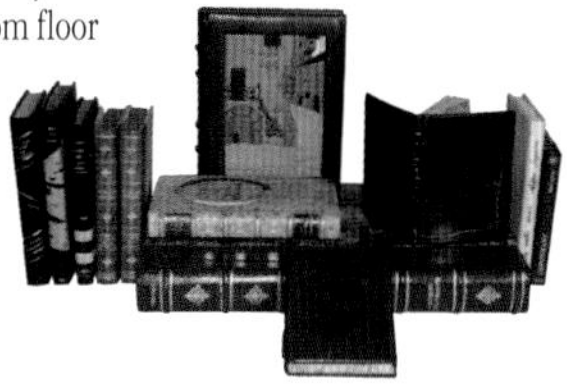

Llibreria Sant Jordi

C. de Ferran, 41
☎ 93 301 18 41
Metro Jaume I or Liceu
Open Mon.-Sat. 9.30am-2pm, 4.30-9pm.
Father and son have run this bookshop since 1880. The *Modernista* decor belongs to a bygone age. A warm welcome and knowledgeable help guide you in your choice of works on art, architecture and design. Out of curiosity, take a look at the charming *calendari dels pagesos*, astronomical and religious calendars, littered with nursery rhymes and sayings (€1.20).

BOOK AND MAGAZINE PUBLISHING

Barcelona is really the center of the publishing industry in Spain and the bulk of the printers, papermills and publishers are located in and around the city. It's therefore no coincidence that Barcelona has given birth to a large number of publications, magazines and comic-strip books, the latter being very much part of a tradition, if not a way of life in some non-English-speaking European countries.

Gastronomy

However you style yourself – gourmet, Epicurean, bon viveur, or just plain foodie – there is a great deal of scope for trying out new flavors in Barcelona and lots of opportunities to take some of these regional specialties home with you. Here are a few specialist shops for you to try.

Colmado Quilez

Rambla de Catalunya, 63
☎ 93 215 23 56
Open Mon.-Fri. 9am-2pm, 4.30-8.30pm (closed Sat. pm).

A traditional grocer's that has offered a wide choice of high-quality local products for the past 50 years. Bottles and tins are piled from floor to ceiling in a chaotic, old-fashioned but charming way.

Fargas

Plaça Cucurulla, 2
☎ 93 302 03 42
Metro Catalunya
Open Mon.-Sat. 9am-1.30pm, 4-8pm.

The pretty shopfront of this confectioner's, a stone's throw from the cathedral, promises old-fashioned delicacies. They're still made the traditional way, using a millstone to produce powdered drinking chocolate. Among the specialties of the shop are *bombons de tardor*, *catanis* – almond, caramel and chocolate sweets which cost around €32.50 per kg/2.2lb.

Comme-Bio

Via Laietana, 28
☎ 93 319 89 68
Open Mon.-Sun. 9am-11pm.

As you may gather from the name, the products on sale at Comme-Bio exude well-being and health. It sells camomile,

marjoram, thyme, passionflower, organic chocolate, wholemeal bread and beer. You can also try the organic products on the premises.

Caelum

Carrer de la Palla, 8
☎ 93 302 69 93
Open every day 10am-2pm, 5-8.30pm (closed Mon. am and Sun. pm). Restaurant open Tue.-Sat. 5-8.30pm.

A new and highly unusual addition to the antique district, Caelum advertises "monastery delights and temptations." It's an old-fashioned shop which boasts medieval recipes, communion wine and rose-petal jam. All these delicacies are prepared in secret within the confines of the monasteries. You can try out these particularly divine specialties in a cellar occupying a former

14th-century public baths and also admire bed linen embroidered by nuns.

Planelles-Donat

Portal de l'Angel, 25
☎ 93 317 34 39
Metro Catalunya
Open Mon.-Sat. 10am-8pm.
Carrer de Curcurulla, 9
Metro Liceu
Open Mon.-Sat. 10am-2pm, 4-8pm, Sun. 10am-2.30pm.

Since 1870, five generations of the Donat family have sold all kinds of *turrónes* (see box right) in slabs as well as by weight to passersby in the street. The windswept stall gets packed at Christmas time,

when the sweet-toothed people of Barcelona come out to treat themselves. *Turrón* makes an ideal, typically Catalan present to take back home with you.

J. Mùrria

C. de Roger de Lluria, 85
☎ 93 215 57 89
Metro Passeig de Gràcia
Open Mon.-Sat. 10am-2pm, 5-8.30pm.

A visit to J. Mùrria is not only a feast for your taste buds, but also for your eyes. The wonderful selection of goods is displayed in an exceptionally well-preserved *Modernista* setting. Haunches of Guijuelo ham, nuts, extra virgin olive oil, jams and preserves from Penedès – all very tasty treats for a highly refined palate.

La Viniteca

C. dels Agullers, 7
☎ 93 268 32 27
Metro Jaume I
Open Mon.-Sat. 8.30am-2.30pm, 4.30-8.30pm.

La Viniteca overflows with a range of full-bodied red wines (Rioja €3), fruity dry white wines (Penedès €3.60), local sparkling wines (Cava Codorniu brut €6), rosés, spirits, etc.

La Colmena

Plaça de l'Angel, 12
☎ 93 315 13 56
Metro Jaume I
Open Mon.-Sun. 9am-9pm.

La Colmena is one of the few cake shops in the city specializing in sweets and soft caramels flavored with eucalyptus, pine, thyme, fennel and coffee (€9 per kg/2.2lb). Since the beginning of the 20th century, this sweet-shop has sold nougat with crème brûlée (*de biema*), *panellets* in marzipan on All Saints' Day, and treats to sweet-toothed people of all ages.

TURRÓN, BLENDING FLAVORS FROM NORTH AFRICA

The *turrón de Jijona* is an Arabic sweet that's said to date back to the 15th century. Originally from North Africa, it's a subtle blend of Mediterranean flavors – almond, honey and cinnamon. It used to be sold during the three months of the Christmas *ferias*, but in 1850 these fairs ceased to be held and so the *turrón* vendors had to sell on the street instead, where you'll still find them today.

Practicalities

Barcelona is inseparable from its bars and nightlife. Even the designer Mariscal reflected on this when he coined the Catalan play on words, "Bar-cel-ona" (Bar = bar, cel = sky, and ona = wave). All across the city, bars and clubs come alive on a nightly basis. From cocktail lounges to jazz bars, from post-modern decor to disused hangars, you can listen and dance to every conceivable beat. Be prepared to be intoxicated by it all and party into the early hours.

Where and when?

Barcelona nightlife is constantly changing. Trendy places are quickly replaced by new names, and cafés and bars succeed each other at an alarming rate. The people of Barcelona love going out; all age groups, all night and all year round. It's very difficult to recommend one district more than another because the hot spots vary according to the season.
As you might expect, Thursday, Friday and Saturday nights are most popular. In summer, *carpas* (marquees) are erected in the port or stadiums, or even on the city heights.

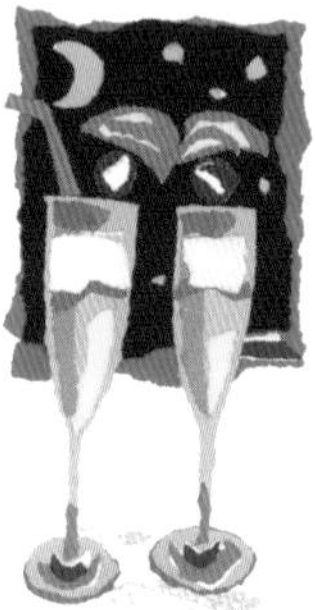

Always spectacular, they have the best bars of the season, and are definitely not to be missed.

How much?

It's quite usual to only have to pay for your drinks, which makes it possible to move from place to place without seriously damaging your budget. If you have to pay to get into a club the price usually varies between €6-12, but the first drink is often free, or the person accompanying you may get in free.
Cinema tickets are cheap

GETTING AROUND

Use taxis to get from place to place – they're affordable and available in vast numbers. The city is generally safe, except for the Barrio Chino (Chinatown), an area notorious for drugs and prostitution. Take a taxi if you go there after dark.

(around €4.20, whereas theater tickets cost around €12).

Some dos and don'ts

Don't set off too early – most bars are dead before 11pm. It's also wise not to turn up at some of the clubs until 2am, otherwise you're likely to be the only person there! If the partying goes on until dawn, there'll always a bar to serve you *chocolate con churros* or a baker's to cut up a crispy *pa de coca* to keep you going. By then, you'll have discovered that Barcelona rarely sleeps. The life of the hard-working, hard-playing Catalan can be yours, provided you can keep up with it.

How to make reservations

If you want to make a last-minute booking for a concert or show, your hotel porter will help you, but you'll need to have an idea of what you want to see or you may end up saddled with his choice. You can get information from *la Guia del Ocio*, and the *El Pais* and *la Vanguardia* newspapers, which will give you the prices and times of performances and the telephone numbers.

For some shows, a 50 percent reduction is available three hours before the start of the performance. Enquire at the Tourist Information Office in the Plaça de Catalunya (see p. 35). Concerts at the Palau de la Musica (see pp. 42-43) are often very popular and seats need to be reserved well in advance. As for the Liceu opera house (see p. 49), it has been rebuilt after burning down for the third time in 1994.

THE BARCELONA LOOK

The discos and night clubs have no specific dress code, so you can wear what you like and if you're really partial to wigs and silk stockings, no one will take offence. Barcelona is much less straight-laced and conventional than Madrid, so don't take too many smart clothes along for the evenings – concerts are really the only opportunities to dress up a little. As for restaurants, the atmosphere everywhere is very relaxed.

Bars...

1 - La Bolsa
2 - Un Coche Menys
3 - Universal (p. 133)

Tapas bars and late snacks

L'Arquer

Gran Via de les Corts Catalanes, 454
☎ 93 423 99 08
Metro Rocafort
Open Tue.-Sun. 7pm-3am.

Tapas, copas y flechas, or how to pass an evening playing at Robin Hood! Four Olympic archery ranges (€7.20 for half an hour) allow you to demonstrate your great skill, while nonchalantly sipping on a "magic-potion" cocktail.

La Bolsa

C. de Tuset, 17
☎ 93 202 26 35
Metro Diagonal
Open Mon.-Fri. 8.30pm-3am, Sat.-Sun. 6pm-3am.

This bar has an innovative pricing system. Set up to work like the stockmarket, drinks are quoted like commodities and prices, displayed on screens, fluctuate according to the amounts consumed. It is an attractive brick and wood-panelled setting where you can watch your whisky on the rise!

Sukür

C. Avinyó, 42
☎ 93 301 01 02
Metro Liceu
Open Mon.-Sat. 11am-2am, Sun 5pm-1am; Restaurant until 4.30pm and from 9pm.

The restaurant-cocktail bar-boutique concept reaches Barcelona. People come to Sukür for the refinement of the oriental decoration, its intimate atmosphere – tables are separated from each other by warm colored fabric partitions - its mint tea and Mediteranean specialties such as tuna cooked with ginger, tajine, couscous...You can pick up a piece of Morracan craft or a CD on your way out.

Schilling

C. de Ferran, 23
☎ 93 317 67 87
Open every day 10am-2am.

Not far from the cathedral, this is one of the "in" places. Once an old knife factory, it has been turned into a very popular café. Exposed stonework, subdued lighting and *bistrot* tables make a very cozy setting for a cosmopolitan and gay clientèle. Try to get here around 8pm.

Sagardi

C. Argenteria, 62
☎ 93 319 99 93
Metro Jaume I
Every day until 1am.

One sentence says it all: "extensive selection of hot and cold *tapas*." Simple enough: pick your *tapas* at the bar, eat them inside or outside, and pay on the way out according to the number of picks left on your plate. A highly popular spot – Sagardi caters to all tastes. You can also ask for a liqueur from the vast collection, or treat yourself to a delicious dessert.

The Quiet Man

C. del Marqués de Barbera, 11
☎ 93 412 12 19
Open every day 6pm-2.30am.

Feeling nostalgic for an old Irish pub? Even in Barcelona you'll be able to drink a pint of foaming Guinness or a pure malt whisky in an Irish setting, with Celtic music at the weekend.

La Vinya del Senyor

Plaça Santa Maria, 5
☎ 93 310 33 79
Open Tue.-Sun. noon-1am.

Located on a charming square, this bar has one of the most pleasant terraces in the city. Enjoy local wines on candlelit tables, seated under the vines that give the bar its name. A delightful spot.

Casa Fernandez

C. de Santaló, 46
☎ 93 201 93 08
Metro Diagonal
Open every day 1pm-1.30am.

If you suddenly feel hungry in the course of your nighttime wanderings, try Casa Fernandez for a quick bite, where you can sample a selection of cold sausages and hams or a creamy *tortilla* washed down with the local Penedès wine. You'll soon be ready for more!

Vildsvin

C. Ferran, 38
☎ 93 317 94 07
Metro Jaume I
Restaurant: Mon.-Thu. until midnight, (weekend 1am); bar: until 2am.

In this refined setting, halfway between a local eatery and a Japanese sushi bar, you can choose between champagne and beer, traditional dishes and succulent duck wing *tapas*. The crowd is composed of intellectuals, bankers, artists and aesthetes. Booking is recommended on weekends. If you feel like eating oysters in the middle of the night, this is also a good place. Vildsvin also serves breakfast.

El Salon

C. de l'Hostal d'En Sol, 6
☎ 93 315 21 59
Metro Jaume I
Open Mon.-Sat. 1pm-3am.

El Salon is a friendly bar opening onto a little street behind the post office. It's the cheerful blend of odd chairs and tables, Baroque chandeliers, exposed stonework and a comfortable old sofa that make this an ideal setting for homemade pastries or a warming bowl of vegetable soup until as late as 3am.

El Japones

Passatge de la Concepció, 2
☎ 93 487 25 92
Lunchtime: Mon.-Fri. 1.30-4pm, Sat. & Sun. 1.30-5pm.
Evenings: Sun.-Thu. 8.30pm-midnight, Fri.-Sat. 8.30pm-1am.

Enjoy delicious Japanese food in a trendy Zen environment seated at large shared tables with wooden benches. The kitchen opens onto the dining area so you can watch the chefs at work.

Escribà

Litoral Mar, 42, Platja del Bogatell
☎ 93 221 07 29
Metro Ciutadella or take a taxi
Open Tue.-Fri. 1.-4.30pm, Sat. noon-6pm, Sun. noon-11pm.

Since 1906 Escribà has specialized in homemade sweets and

UN COCHE MENYS

C. de Esparteria, 3
☎ 93 268 21 05
Open Sat.-Sun. set off 10am, return 12.30pm, Tue. and Sat. set off 8.30pm, return midnight.

How to explore the city, stay fit and help protect the environment. On Tuesday and Saturday evenings dozens of people set off on bicycles in pursuit of a guide, criss-crossing the city in all directions. Aperitifs and dinner are included and afterwards there's dancing. It's a good, easy way to get to know the Catalans and a few unusual places. All you need is a passport and the right sportswear.

pastries – praline-flavored chocolates and bitter chocolate cream slices – washed down with a cup of Ethiopian coffee. In this *chiringuito* (seaside restaurant) there are plenty of mouthwatering dishes for you to try.

All-night bars

Reñé

Consell de Cent, 362-364
☎ 93 488 27 71
Metro Passeig de Gràcia or Girona
Every day 8am-2pm, closed Sun. night.

Brand new Reñé has moved into this ancient pastry shop (which originally bore the name), keeping the modernist façade and some of its more remarkable internal architectural details. The rest isvery much inspired by Italian design. Next to the fusion food restaurant is a chill-out-zone for cocktail drinkers and cigar smokers.

LONDON BAR

Nou de la Rambla, 34
☎ 93 318 52 61
Metro Liceu
Open Tue.-Sun. 7pm-4am.

The Raval district (beware of pickpockets) has fortunately preserved this bar, which opened in 1910 and where Picasso used to come on his nightly wanderings. The decor with the patina of time, tobacco smoke and jazz rhythms are reminders of the former Bohemian lifestyle. On some evenings, a trapeze artist whirls through the air in memory of the artists of the Barcelonés circus, which was destroyed during the Civil War.

Síncopa

C. Avinyó, 35
Metro Drassanes ou Jaume I
Open every day 6pm-2am (Fri. & Sat. until 3am)

Here is a warm and welcoming place to stop at on your nocturnal strolls between the cathedral and the Moll de la Fusta. It serves tequila sunrises and margaritas to fans of the Brazilian and Carribean way of life. Whether you stay at the bar or stray in the crowded little room, this red-and-yellow night spot is the ideal place to share a drink listening to Latin American music.

Le Marsella

C. de Sant Pau, 65
☎ 93 442 73 63
Metro Liceu
Open Mon.-Thu. 9pm-2.30am, Fri.-Sun. 6pm-2.30am.

Indiana Jones would feel quite at home in this bar, located in the Raval district. Its original decor, old mirrors, *bistrot* chairs and marble tables create quite a nostalgic atmosphere. On the weekends a fortune-teller will read the cards for you.

Snooker

C. de Roger de Llúria, 42
☎ 93 317 97 60
Metro Urquinaona
Open every day 6pm-3am.

A splendid red-and-gold decor, with subdued alabaster lights, Riart armchairs dotted around and, as you might imagine, a number of snooker players. A stylish setting for a mojito or Hawaiian cocktail.

Zsa-Zsa

C. de Rosselló, 156 (C1)
☎ 93 453 85 66
Metro Diagonal
Open Mon.-Sat. 9pm-3am.

The kilim-covered walls are a blaze of color, and together with the studied lighting and pale birchwood partitions, the decor adds a touch of magic to the place. You can sip a cocktail at the bar on a tall metal stool while listening to the salsa rhythms, which complete the atmosphere.

Dot

Nou de Sant Francesc, 7
☎ 93 302 70 26
Metro Drassanes
Open Mon.Thu. 10pm-2.30am, Fri.-Sun. 10pm-3am.

One of the best places to come for a night out, with a great DJ and film shows projected on the dance floor. A trendy place you shouldn't miss that's full to bursting every weekend. *Buenas copas y muchas risas* – good drinks and plenty of laughter.

Insolit

Moll d'Espanya
Maremagnum, L111
☎ 93 225 81 78
Metro Barceloneta
Open Mon.-Sun. 1-11pm, nightclub until 5am.

With its futuristic decor, this cybercafé is an Internet bar for late nights on the web. Half an hour's connection to anywhere in the world costs €3.60.

Tres Torres

Via Augusta, 300
☎ 93 205 16 08
Funicular Tres Torres
Open Mon.-Thu. 5pm-3am, Fri.-Sat. until 4am.

In summer, the terraces and garden of this splendid *Modernista* villa turn it into a magical place, with little tables and bamboo armchairs set out under the palm trees. It's the ideal place to sip a glass of punch in the moonlight.

1 - Snooker
2 - Otto Zutz (p. 133)
3 - La Fira

Almirall

C. de Joaquin Costa, 33
☎ 93 412 15 35
Metro Liceu
Open every day 8pm-2am.

Only a short walk from the Museum of Contemporary Art, this bar in the Raval has kept its original *Modernista* setting. Local regulars congregate round the little *bistrot* tables or sit on the battered sofas.

LA FIRA

C. de Provença, 171
Metro Hospital Clinic
Open Mon.-Thu. 1pm-midnight, Fri.-Sun. 1pm-5am.

If you're nostalgic for the atmosphere of La Strada, you'll love the La Fira bar. An enthusiast brought the bric-a-brac of a disused funfair here piece by piece – distorting mirrors, arcade machines, a fortune-teller, trapezes and roundabouts, all with a tale to tell. For those who love poetry in motion.

Mirablau

Avinguda de Tibidabo
☎ 93 418 58 79
At the foot of the funicular.
Open every day 11-5am.

This bar, with its panoramic view, is a must to round off a romantic evening. From 2am onward, couples gather on the terrace and gaze at the lights of the city twinkling in the distance. A timeless classic.

La Morera

C. Fossar de les Moreres, 5
☎ 93 315 29 60
Metro Jaume I or Barceloneta
Open until midnight during the week, 2am during the weekend.

A bodega-bar serving exquisite wines just off the busy Passeig del Born, on the south side of Santa Maria del Mar. Its two floors, with their elegant wooden red interiors and intimate lighting, draw a discrete cosmopolitan crowd. Live jazz on certain evenings.

El Born

Passeig del Born, 79
☎ 93 319 57 11
Metro Jaume I
Open every evening 8pm-12.30am.

The Plaça del Born is *the* place for anyone wanting to spend a night on the town. A tour of the bars is a must, with the El Born, El Copetin and Miramelindo all vying for the favors of those intent on pleasure. You can dance, sip cocktails and set the world to rights until the small hours, if you have the stamina.

Rosebud

C. d'Adria Margarit, 27
Avinguda de Tibidabo
☎ 93 418 88 85
Open Mon.-Fri. 9pm-4am, Sat.-Sun. 7pm-5.30am.

Rosebud takes its name from the last word uttered by the hero of the 1941 movie *Citizen Kane* and doesn't refer to the bar's setting. It's an ideal place to come on a mild summer evening, nevertheless, when the enormous glass dome makes a pleasant setting.

Gimlet

C. del Rec, 24
☎ 93 310 10 27
Open Mon.-Sat. 8pm-3am.

In the 1970s Gimlet put new life into cocktails. The understated decor, with its glass cabinets and wooden bar pays discreet homage to New York cocktail bars of the 1930s. Connoisseurs know they serve the best dry Martinis in the city here.

Torres de Avila

Av. Marquès de Comillas
☎ 93 424 93 09
Metro Espanya
Open Fri.-Sat. 11pm-5am.

Some talented designers have converted the two towers of the entrance to the Pueblo Español. Bars, billiard rooms and terraces decorated with stars by Mariscal are arranged on several levels like a set of Russian dolls. The panoramic view from the rooftop terraces is a must in summer.

LA PALOMA

Carrer de Tigre, 27
☎ 93 301 68 97
Open Thu.-Sun. evenings.

A legendary dance hall with all the charm of yesteryear that's well worth a visit. Everything could be classed as of historical interest here, from the smooth crooners of the orchestra with their greying, slicked-back hair to the stucco ornamentation of the balconies.

Palau Dalmases

C. de Montcada, 20
☎ 93 310 06 73
Metro Jaume I
Open Tue.-Sat. 8pm-2am, Sun. 8-10pm.

A sumptuous Baroque setting in an aristocratic palace on the Montcada, a stone's throw from the Picasso Museum. Gleaming mirrors, the scent of musk, amber and iris, bowls of fresh fruit and garlands of flowers bathed in candlelight turn the weekly concert of Baroque music into a dream.

Café Royale

C. Nou de Zurbano, 3
☎ 93 317 61 2
Metro Liceu
Open Tue.-Thu. 5pm-2.30am, Fri.-Sat. 5pm-3am.

Next to the colonnades of the Plaça Reial, the sofas of the Café Royale have been drawing huge crowds of late. Neither the comfortable sitting arrangements nor its sophisticated design can claim responsibility for the success of this warm, cocoon-like venue: indeed, the main attraction is local DJ Fred Guzzo. His mix of funk, soul, bossa nova, latin music and jazz is getting everybody dancing, no matter where they are, on the sofas or at the bar.

Cabarets, jazz and shows

La Boite

Avinguda Diagonal, 477
☎ 93 419 59 50
Open every day 11pm-5.30am.

Thought to be the best jazz cellar in Barcelona with a 1970s decor and knowledgeable audience, presents legendary artists such as Lou Benett, Dr Feelgood and jazz musicians from all over the world, as well as bands playing funk-jazz, hard-soul, reggae, blues, etc. After the concert, the fevered atmosphere of the disco takes over.

Costa Breve

C. d'Aribau, 230
☎ 93 414 27 78
Open Thu.-Sat. 11pm-5am.

Smart and clean but beginning to show its age, this is one of Barcelona's more trendy places, with something for every musical taste. Take your pick from salsa, rumba, funk, acid-jazz, swing, country and blues.

Tarantos

Plaça Reial, 17
☎ 93 318 30 67
Shows Mon.-Sat. at 10pm
Entry charge €22.84.

Flamenco isn't popular with Catalans, but it you want to see this Andalucian dance during your stay then Los Tarantos are the unrivalled masters of the art. Their singing and

1 - Rosebud (p. 131)
2 - Palau Dalmases
3 - Torres de Avila

guitar playing and the artistry of the dancers make a wonderful show.

Jamboree

Plaça Reial, 17
☎ 93 301 75 64
Open every day 9pm-5am.

Housed in the vaults of a former convent, this was the first jazz club opened in Spain, in 1959. It has long since swapped the cornet for the saxophone, and Dixieland and New-Orleans jazz have made way for the rhythms of funk.

Salsitas

C. Nou de la Rambla, 22
☎ 93 318 08 40
Metro Parallel
Open Tue.-Thu. 8pm-2.30am, Fri.-Sat. 8pm-4am, Sun. 8pm-2.30am.

An interesting and original venue, with white decor, that serves Mediterranean cuisine. At midnight it's transformed into one of the trendiest clubs in the city, with house music played by a cool DJ. The atmosphere is pretty wild, so put on your glad rags and dance the night away.

Nightclubs and discos

Universal

C. de Maria Cubí, 182
☎ 93 201 35 96
Open Mon.-Sat. 10pm-4.30am.

Opened in 1985 this is still the trendiest place in Barcelona, but beware of the decibel level. This is a classic bar with designer decor. There are always lines to get in, but they are quite choosey about who they will admit.

Otto Zutz

C. de Lincoln, 15
☎ 93 238 07 22
Open Tue.-Sat. from midnight.

Located in an old warehouse, this club has six bars and an enormous dance floor on three levels. Hopeful entrants are vetted at the door– you'll only get in if they like the look of you. An interesting mix, from football stars to artists and designers. They sometimes have bands playing live here.

Bikini Club

Deu i Mata, 105
☎ 93 322 00 05
Tue.-Sun. from 11.30pm.

Under the Illa center, 1,200sq m (13,000sq ft) of floor space on two levels house a concert hall, a dance floor and a calm lounge for quiet conversation. After falling into decline, this legendary Barcelona nightspot has risen from the ashes more vibrant than ever.

Up and Down

C. de Numancia, 179
☎ 93 205 51 94
Open Tue.-Sat. from midnight.

The place to come if you're with your parents – upstairs for them and downstairs for you. It's how the Barcelona middle classes solve the generation gap. Wear a tie and dine to music upstairs, or wear what you like and have soft drinks downstairs.

Luz de Gas

C. de Muntaner, 246
☎ 93 209 77 11
Open Fri.-Sat. until 6am, Sun. 10pm, opera concerts.

This former Belle-Epoque theater has been turned into an enormous dance and concert hall, with the upper gallery a pleasant place for a quiet chat or tasty *bocadillo* (Spanish-style sandwich). The clientele ranges from 7 to 77.

Mirabé

C. de Manuel Arnús, 2
☎ 93 434 00 35
Open every day 7am-3am.

Have a drink in the romantic garden with its panoramic view over Barcelona. This music bar is located on the city heights and is a trendy venue for well-heeled and glamorous regulars. It's quiet and intimate on the first floor, but if you fancy dancing the night away to your favorite tunes from the 1980s, head downstairs.

LLIURE THEATER

C. del Montseny, 47
☎ 93 218 92 51
Metro Fontana
Open Tue.-Sun.

Since 1976, this former cooperative has been home to the prestigious "Free Theater," with performances strictly in Catalan. You can always get round the language barrier by opting to see a performance of contemporary dance instead of a play.

Music

L'Auditori

C. de Lepant, 150
☎ 93 247 93 00
www.auditori.com
Credit card ticket sales:
☎ 902 10 12 12

This building, designed by the architect Rafael Moneo, opened in 1999, and with its perfect acoustics, has become a reference point in the world of classical music, satisfying even the most demanding of music lovers. It has two concert rooms – not to be missed.

Palau de la Musica

C. de Sant Francesc de Paula, 2
☎ 93 295 72 00
Metro Urquinaona.

If you're a classical music lover, find out what's on the program at this magnificent concert hall as soon as you arrive in the city. The splendid *Modernista* decor by Domenech i Montaner is also worthy of close attention (see pp. 42-43, Ribera).

Places not to miss in the Barrio de Gràcia

We recommend a tour of one of the city's most popular districts, the Barrio de Gràcia, which is little-frequented by tourists. Spared by the rebuilding for the Olympics, it retains much of its original charm. This former suburb has preserved its character thanks to its squares, covered markets, cafés and the Lliure theater. Leave the metro at Fontana station and follow our guide.

Sol Soler

Plaça del Sol, 13
☎ 93 217 44 40
Open Mon.-Tue. 7pm-midnight, Wed.-Sun. noon-midnight.

On the Plaça del Sol, there ar at least half a dozen bar occupying the terraces. T start the evening, you can tr mouthwatering *tapas* – chicken wings in sweet an sour sauce, tabbouleh wit fresh herbs, and vegetable an fish pâté. *Bistrot* tables checkered tiles, and whirrin fans set the scene for tasty foo and local wines.

Virreina

Plaça Virreina, 1
☎ 93 237 98 80
Open every day 10am-1.30am.

There's a village atmosphere o the terrace, located on one of th

prettiest squares in the area Families enjoy it here a lunchtime, but it gets more livel in the evening, particularly be fore or after a film in the nearb Verdi cinema.

Tons

C. dels Xiquets de Valls, 14
☎ 93 237 78 20
Open Mon.-Sat. 10am-2pm 5-8.30pm.

This is an inspirational place fo those interested in interio

1 - Salsitas (p. 133)
2 - L'Auditori
3 - Snooker (p. 130)

decoration. They sell lights, lampshades and doorknobs in original shapes and colors. If you want to try your hand at some decorative painting there are paints, brushes and stencils. They also have an interesting line of table linen.

Café del Sol

Plaça del Sol, 16
☎ 93 415 56 63
Open every day 1pm-2.30am.

Sit on the terrace of the bar and see what's going on in the square – old people gossiping and taking a walk in their slippers, children playing ball and young couples smooching happily on the benches. It is a great place to relax and watch the world go by.

Bodega Manolo

C. de Torrent de les Flors, 101
☎ 93 284 43 77
Open for lunch Tue.-Sat., dinner Thu.-Sat.

A truly authentic, traditional *bodega*, where you sit at a neon-lit bar to drink the local wine, unless you happen to have brought along a bottle to fill from one of the barrels. If you have time, have a plate of grilled green asparagus, tuna carpaccio and grilled cuttlefish with mushrooms. With the locals all around you, it's a slice of Barcelona life to savor to the full.

Sabor Cubano

C. Francesco Giner, 32
☎ 93 217 35 41
Open every day 9pm-3am.

After a warm welcome, you'll feel as if you've just landed in the Caribbean. On Wednesday evenings a live orchestra invites you to step into the spotlight and dance to the salsa beat. All the flavor of Cuba right here in the Gràcia.

Fronda

C. de Verdi, 15
☎ 93 415 20 55
Open every day exc. Tue. 8pm-1am (to 3am at weekends).

Close to the Verdi cinema, one of the few places to show films in the original language, Fronda takes pride in its appearance, with a mahogany bar, subdued lighting, rattan armchairs and tables, a relaxed atmosphere and a jazz accompaniment.

Metric Conversion Chart

Women's sizes

Shirts/dresses

U.K	U.S.A	EUROPE
8	6	36
10	8	38
12	10	40
14	12	42
16	14	44
18	16	46

Sweaters

U.K	U.S.A	EUROPE
8	6	44
10	8	46
12	10	48
14	12	50
16	14	52

Shoes

U.K	U.S.A	EUROPE
3	5	36
4	6	37
5	7	38
6	8	39
7	9	40
8	10	41

Men's sizes

Shirts

U.K	U.S.A	EUROPE
14	14	36
14½	14½	37
15	15	38
15½	15½	39
16	16	41
16½	16½	42
17	17	43
17½	17½	44
18	18	46

Suits

U.K	U.S.A	EUROPE
36	36	46
38	38	48
40	40	50
42	42	52
44	44	54
46	46	56

Shoes

U.K	U.S.A	EUROPE
6	8	39
7	9	40
8	10	41
9	10.5	42
10	11	43
11	12	44
12	13	45

More useful conversions

1 centimeter	0.39 inches	1 inch	2.54 centimeters
1 meter	1.09 yards	1 yard	0.91 meters
1 kilometer	0.62 miles	1 mile	1. 61 kilometers
1 liter	1.76 pints	1 pint	0.57 liters
1 gram	0.035 ounces	1 ounce	28.35 grams
1 kilogram	2.2 pounds	1 pound	0.45 kilograms

A

airport to the city center: **8**
Alexandra, Hotel: **86-87**
Ample, Carrer: **8**
Antiques and antique shops: **20-21, 114-115**
Arc de Triomf: **57**
Arcades, shopping: **106-107**
Art galleries: **118-119**
Arts Barcelona Hotel: **76**
Arts Hotel: **62**
Azuléjos: **21, 115**

B

Barça Soccer Club: **18-19**
Barça Museum: **19**
Barceloneta: **60-63**
Barrio Chino: **47**
Barrio de Gràcia: **134**
Barrio Gótico: **38-41, 87, 90**
Bars: **13, 85, 128-132**
Bookshops: **122-123**
Boqueria (market): **49**
Budget: **7**
Bulevard Rosa shopping center: **107**
Buses: **33**

C

Cabaret: **132-133**
Cafés & tea rooms: **94-95**
Caixa de nuvia: **20, 21**
Calatrava Tower: **67**
Call, The: **41**
Car rental: **33-34**
Camp Nou: **19, 108**
Casa Calvet: **53**
Casa Milà: **53, 90-91**
Castell de Montjuïc: **69**
Catalonia Excursion Centre: **39**
Cathedral: **37, 38-39, 80**
Centre de Cultura Contemporánia de Barcelona (CCCB): **46**
Cerdà, Idelfons: **55**
Cervantès House: **59**
Chapel of St. Agatha: **40**
Children's clothes/games shops: **104-105**
Chiringuitos: **13, 63**
Christopher Columbus Monument: **58**
Churches:
Betlem: **48-49**
Del Pi: **40**
La Mercè: **59**
Santa Maria del Mar: **43**
St. Miquel del Port: **61**
City heights: **92**
Ciutadella: **56-57**
Claris, Hotel: **87**
Clubs: **133-134**
Coach: **6-7**
Colon, Hotel: **73**
Condes de Barcelona, Hotel: **87**
Conversion tables: **139**
Craft shops: **120-121**
Cultural Center of the Caixa Palau Macaya Foundation: **119**
Customs: 8

D

Department stores: **106-107**
Design and design shops: **24-27, 110-113**
Diagonal, Avinguda: **65**
Diagonal Pedralbes: **64-65, 88**
Diocesan Museum: **39**
Discos: **133-134**
Drassanes: **58-59**
Duques de Bergara, Hotel: **87**

E

Ecology – shops: **120-121**
Eixample: **52-55, 86-87, 90-91**
El Bulevard dels Antiquaris (shopping centre): **114**
El Corte Inglés shopping centre: **106**
El Triangle shopping centre: **107**
El Xalet Hotel: **71, 89**
Els Encants (fleamarket): **20, 100**
Embassies: **8-9**
Església de Betlem (church): **48-49**
Església de La Mercè: **59**
Església de Sant Miguel del Port: **61**
España Hotel: **89**
Estacio de França: **56**
Euro: **7**

F

Fashion shops: **98-103**
Festivals and traditions: **14-17**
Finca Güell: **65**
Flea markets: **20, 114-115**
Flights: **4-5**
Food and drink: **10-13, 49, 124-125**
Fountain of Canaletes: **19**
Fundació Antoni Tàpies: **36, 53-54, 76**
Fundació Joan Miró: **37, 68, 78**

G

Gadgets: **108-109**
Galerie Maeght: **44**
Gastronomy – shops: **124-125**
Gaudí, Antoni: **30-31, 53, 63**
Gehry, Frank – whale: **62**
Golondrinas, Las: **59**
Gran Derby Hotel: **88**
Gran Hotel Havana: **72**
Gran Teatre de Liceu: **49**
Güell family: **31**

H

Health: **9**
Hobbies and collections – shops: **116-117**
Hospital de la Santa Creu: **47**
Hotel Montecarlo: **88**
Hotels: **84-89**

I

INEFC: **68**
Insurance: **9**
Interior decoration – shops: **110-113**

J

Jardi Hotel: **87**
Jardíns de Pedralbes: **64**

L

Liceu Opera House: **49**
L'Illà shopping centre: **107**
Llancà, Carrer de: **66**
Lliure Theatre: **134**
Llotja, La: **43**

M

Manzana de la Discordia: **53**
Maremagnum shopping centre: **106-107**
Marina Port Vell: **60-61**
Mercado de Numismatica y Filatelia (coin and stamp market): **117**

Mercat Gotic (antiques market): **114**
Mercat Sant Antoni (fleamarket): **114-115**
Mercè, Carrer de la: **59**
Méridien Barcelona Hotel: **88**
Metro: **33**, *inside front cover (map)*
Metropol Hotel: **87**
Miles Van der Rohe Pavilion: **66-67**
Military Museum: **69**
Mirador de l'Alcalde: **68**
Miró, Antonio: **27, 55**
Miró, Joan: **68, 78**
Modernisme *(Modernista)*: **22-23**
Moll d'Espanya: **59**
Moll de la Fusta: **59**
Moll dels Pescadors: **61**
Money: **7**
Montjuïc: **66-67**
Monestir de Pedralbes: **64-65**
MNAC (Museu Nacional d'Art de Catalunya): **36, 68, 75**
Mossen Gardens: **68**
Museu Cau Ferrat: **70-71**
Museu d'Art Contemporani: **36, 47, 74**
Museu d'Art Modern de Catalunya: **57**
Museu d'Història Catalunya: **58**
Museu d'Història de la Ciutat: **36, 40-41**
Museu de la Música: **52-53**
Museu de Zoologia: **57**
Museu du Tèxtil i d'Indumentària: **43**
Museu Frederic Marès: **40**
Museu Maricel: **71**
Museu Marítim: **58-59**
Museu Picasso: **36, 43, 73**
Museu Romàntic: **71**
Museum opening times: **35**
Music venues: **132-134**

N

Nightlife: **126-135**
Nouvel Hotel: **87**
Nova Icària: **62-63**

O

Office accessories – shops: **122-123**
Olympic Stadium and Galería: **67**
Oriente, Hotel: **49**

P

Palau de la Música: **37, 42-43, 82**
Palau de la Virreina: **49**
Palau de Mar: **61**
Palau de Pedralbes: **64**
Palau Güell: **47**
Palau Sant Jordi: **67**
Parc de la Ciutadella Umbracle/Hivernacle: **57**
Parc Güell: **30, 83**
Parc Zoològic: **57**
Passeig de Gràcia: **52**
Passeig de la Ribera: **70**
Passeig del Born: **43**
Passeig Marítim: **62**
Pia Almoina: **39**
Picasso, Pablo: **28-29, 43**
Picornell swimming pools: **68**
Plaça de Braus les Arenes: **66**
Plaça de Catalunya: **48**
Pla de la Garsa: **44**
Plaça de Sant Felip Neri: **39**
Plaça de Sant Jaume: **40**
Plaça del Rei: **40**
Plaça del Pi: **40**
Plaça Reial: **49-50**
Plaça Nova: **38**
Poble Espanyol: **67**
Port: **58-59, 91-92**
Port Olímpic: **60-63, 86**
Post office: **34**

Q

Quatre Gats Café: **29**

R

Rambla de Mar: **57**
Ramblas: **48-51, 88, 93**
Raval: **46-47, 88-89, 93**
Rec Contal: **45**
Regencia Colon Hotel: **87**
Restaurants: **85, 90-93**
Rey Juan Carlos 1 Hotel: **88**
Ribera: **42-45, 92-93**
Ritz, Hotel: 86
Rivoli Ramblas, Hotel: **88**
Romàntic Hotel: **89**
Rusiñol, Santiago: **71**

S

Sagrada Família, La: **31, 37, 79**
Saló del Tinell: **40**
San Sebastian Hotel: **89**
Sant Agusti Hotel: **88-89**
Santa Maria del Mar (church): **37, 43, 81**
Santa Maria del Pi: **40**
Santa Monica Art Center: **50**
Sant Pau del Camp Monastery: **47**
Sardana: **17**
Secondhand shops: **114-115**
Set Portes restaurant: **57**
Shoe Museum: **39**
Shopping: **96-97**
Shops: **98-125**
Sitges: **70-71, 89, 93**
Soccer: **18-19**
Sports goods – shops: **108-109**
St. Moritz Hotel: **87**

T

Tableware – shops: **110-113**
Tapas: **12-13**
Tàpies, Antoni: **29, 53-54, 76**
Taxis: **7, 34, 127**
Teatre Grec: **69**
Telephoning: **34**
Textiles: **111**
Thyssen-Bornemisza Collection: **36, 65, 77**
Tibidabo: **65**
Time: **9**
Tourist information offices: **8, 35**
Train: **6, 7, 34**
Transport – getting around: **32-35**
Transport – getting there: **4-5**

U

Universitat: **54**

V

Voltage: **6**

W

Websites: **8**

Z

Zoo: **57**

Published by AA Travel Publishing.

First published as Un grand week-end à Barcelone: © Hachette Livre (Hachette Tourisme), 2004
Written by Marie-Ange Demory, Virginia Pulm and Gaëlle Redon
Maps within the book © Hachette Tourisme

Published by AA Publishing, a trading name of Automobile Association Developments Limited, whose registered office is Fanum House, Basing View, Basingstoke, Hampshire RG21 4EA. Registered number 1878835.

ISBN-10: 0-7495-4835-5
ISBN-13: 978-0-7495-4835-3

Original English translation by Christine Bainbridge and Anthony Moinet © Hachette Livre (Hachette Tourisme), 2005
Additional translation work by G and W Advertising and Publishing © Automobile Association Developments Limited 2006

Cover design by Bookwork Creative Associates, Hampshire
Cover maps produced from map data © 1998–2005 Navigation Technologies BV. All rights reserved.

Colour separation by Kingsclere Design and Print
Printed and bound in China by Leo Paper Products

Cover credits

Front cover : AA World Travel Library/Steve L Day; **Back cover** : Laurent Parrault

Picture credits

Laurent Parrault: p. 2, 3, 10 (t.r., b.l.), 11, 12 (t.r., c.c., b.r.), 13 (c.l., b.r.), 14, 15, 16 (t.l., b.l.), 17 (t.l., c.), 18, 19, 20, 21 (t.l., b.), 22 (t.r., b.c.), 23 (b.l., b.r., c.r.), 24 (t.r.), 25 (b.c., c.l.), 28 (c.l., t.r. J.Miró © ADAGP, Paris 1997), 29 (t.r., c.l., b.c.), 30, 31, 37, 38, 39 (t.r.), 40 (b.r.), 41, 42 (b.l., b.c.), 43 (t.c., b.c.), 44 (b.l., c.r.), 45 (t.l., c.c.), 46 (t.r.), 47 (c.l., b.l., b.r.), 48 (b.l.), 49 (b.r., t.r.), 50, 51 (b.c.), 52 (t.r., t.l., b.r.), 53 (t.c., c.l., b.r.), 54 (c.r.), 55 (t.l., t.c., b.r.), 56, 57, 58, 59, 60, 61 (t.l., t.r.), 62 (c.c., b.l.), 63 (t.l., c.l., c.c., b.r.), 64, 65 (b.r., c.r.), 66, 67 (t.l. © J. Miró, ADAGP, Paris 1997, b.l.), 68 (b.l., b.r.), 69 (c.l., b.c.), 76 (b.l.), 78 (c.c.), 79 (c.c., b.l., b.r.), 80 (c.l.), 81 (c.r.), 84 (t.r., c.r.), 85 (b.l.),86 (t.c., b.l.), 88, 89, 90 (t.r., b.r.), 91 (t.c., t.r., c.l.), 92 (t.r.), 93 (b.r., b.l.), 94, 95, 96 (t.r.), 98, 100 (t.c., b.r.), 101 (b.c.), 102 (t.r., b.r.), 104, 105 (b.c.), 106 (t.r., b.l.), 107 (t.l.), 108, 109 (c.r.), 110 (t.r., c.l., b.l.), 111 (t.l., c.c., b.r.), 114 (t.l., b.r.), 115, 117, 118 (b.l.), 119 (t.l.), 120, 121 (t., c.c.), 122, 124, 125, 126, 127, 128, 129, 130, 131, 132, 133, 134, 135, 136, 137. **Christian Sarramon**: p. 10 (c.r.), 12 (c.l.), 13 (t.l., c.r.), 16 (t.r.), 17 (b.r.), 22 (c.l.), 23 (t.c.), 24 (b.l., b.r.), 25 (t.l.), 29 (b.r. © J. Miró, ADAGP, Paris 1997), 36, 39 (b.c., c.l., b.r.), 40 (c.l.), 42 (c.c.), 44 (c.l.), 45 (b.r.), 46 (b.l.), 47 (t.r.), 48 (c.c., b.r.), 49 (t.l., b.l.), 51 (t.c., c.r.), 52 (c.r.), 54 (b.l.), 55 (c.r., b.l.), 61 (c.l., c.r., b.r.), 62 (b.r.), 63 (t.r.), 65 (c.c., c.l., t.r.), 67 (t.r.), 68 (c.r.), 69 (t.r., b.r.), 78 (b.r.), 84 (b.r), 85 (t.r.), 90 (b.l.), 91 (c.c., b.r.), 92 (c.l., b.c.), 96 (b.c.), 97 (c.c., b.r.), 100 (c.r., b.l.), 101 (t.r., c.l.), 102 (c.l.), 107 (b.l., b.r.), 111 (b.l.), 116 (b.), 118 (t.r.), 119 (b.l.). **Éric Guillot**: p.96 (c.l.), 106 (c.c.). **Hachette Livre**: p. 28 (b.r. © succession Picasso, Paris 1997), 40 (t.r. © succession Picasso, Paris 1997), 42 (t.r. © ADAGP, Paris 1997. **C. Sarramon/Maison de Marie-Claire**: p. 16 (c.r.) **Arca de l'Avia**: p. 21 (c.r.). **Boutique BD**: p. 25 (c.r.). **Karin Wagner**: p. 26 (t.r.). **Ana Hagopian**: p. 26 (c.r.). **Chelo Sastre**: p. 26 (b.). **Ruth**: p. 27 (t.c.). **Nani Marquina**: p. 27 (c.l.). **Antonio Miró**: p. 27 (b.c.). **Clara Uslé**: p. 27 (b.r.). **Ici et La**: p. 43 (b.l.). **Moska**: p. 43 (c.r.). **Gran Teatre del Liceu © Antoni Bofill**: p. 47 (c.c.). **Fundació Caixa Catalunya © Pau Giralt-Miracle**: p. 51 (t.l.). **Tinçon**: p. 52 (b.l.). **Restaurant Tragaluz**: p. 53 (t.l.). **Hotel Arts Barcelona**: p. 72 (t.l.). **Hotel Condes de Barcelona**: p. 72 (c.r.). **Hotel Claris:** p. 72 (b.l.). **Hotel Metropol:** p. 73 (t.r.). **Hotel Gran Derby**: p. 74 (c.l.). **Hotel Montecarlo**: p. 74 (t.r.). **Hotel Rivoli Ramblas**: p. 74 (b.l.). **Hotel Romàntic**: p. 75. **Semproniana**: p. 76 (b.r.). **Reial Club Maritim**: p. 77 (t.r.). **Flash Flash © Leolpoldo Pomés**: p. 77 (c.l.). **La Balsa**: p. 78 (b.l.). **Agua © Jordi Sarrá Arau**: p. 79 (t.r.). **Taxidermista**: p. 80 (c.r.). **La Estrella Sitges**: p. 81 (b.r.). **Forum**: p. 84 (b.l.). **Groc**: p. 85 (t.l.). **Lydia Delgado © Ugo Camera**: p. 85 (b.r.). **Noténom**: p. 86 (b.r.). **Rafa Teja Atelier**: p. 87 (t.r.). **Hipótesi**: p. 87 (c.l.). **Cristina Castañer**: p. 87 (b.l.). **Rosa y Francesc**: p. 87 (b.r.). **Bulevard Rosa:** p. 92 (c.r.). **L'Illà:** p. 93 (t.l.). **Entre Telas:** p. 97 (t.l.). **Arkitectura**: p. 99 (t.l.). **Vinçon**: p. 99 (c.). **Rosa Cortés Interiors**: p. 101 (c.r.).**Hobby Art Center**: p. 103 (t.l., b.c.). **Editiones T**: p. 105 (t.l.). **La Caixa**: p. 105 (c.r.). **Cereria Subirà**: p. 107 (c.r.). **Tarlatana**: p. 109 (b.). **La Central © Eva Bellapart**: p. 109 (t.l.). **Caelum**: p. 110 (b.r.). **L'Auditori © Roger Velázquez**: p. 121 (b.l.).

Illustrations

Pascal Garnier

A02680